Natacha Lescaille Elias

Interprofessional education and collaborative practice in health

Natacha Lescaille Elias

Interprofessional education and collaborative practice in health

Postgraduate academic and research view, through a multidisciplinary pedagogical collective

ScienciaScripts

Imprint

Cover image: www.ingimage.com

This book is a translation from the original published under ISBN 978-620-2-10536-1.

Publisher:
Sciencia Scripts
is a trademark of
Dodo Books Indian Ocean Ltd. and OmniScriptum S.R.L publishing group

120 High Road, East Finchley, London, N2 9ED, United Kingdom
Str. Armeneasca 28/1, office 1, Chisinau MD-2012, Republic of Moldova, Europe
Printed at: see last page
ISBN: 978-620-5-65412-5

THEORETICAL, CONCEPTUAL AND METHODOLOGICAL BASES OF INTERPROFESSIONAL EDUCATION AND COLLABORATIVE PRACTICE IN THE HEALTH SECTOR IN CUBA

Viewed from the academic postgraduate level and research, through a multidisciplinary pedagogical collective.

01/01/2023

MINISTRY OF PUBLIC HEALTH

Dr.C. Natacha **Lesc** a ill e **Elias**. Graduate in Health Technology, specialized in Medical Imaging. Master in Educational Sciences, Master of Technical and Professional Education. D. in Medical Education Sciences. Professor. Researcher. National Professor of Health Technology. Directorate of Medical Teaching of the Ministry of Public Health of Cuba.

TABLE OF CONTENTS

Authors:

Dr. C. Heidi Soca Gonzalez. Medical Specialist of 1st and 2nd degree in Normal and Pathological Physiology. Master of Science in Higher Education. Doctor in Educational Sciences. Full Professor. Head of the Methodological Teaching Department. Directorate of Medical Teaching of the Ministry of Public Health.

MSc. Omar Gonzalez Delgado. Bachelor in Nursing. Master in Emergency Medicine. Assistant Professor. National Methodologist of the Nursing career. Directorate of Medical Teaching of the Ministry of Public Health.

Lic. Ivon Arteman Cremé. Licentiate in Special Education, specialized in Defectology. Assistant Professor. Specialist of the Department of Foreign Scholarship Holders. Directorate of Medical Teaching of the Ministry of Public Health.

MSc. Adis Padilla Rivero. Licentiate in Nursing. Assistant Professor. Master in Primary Health Care. Specialist of the Department of Secretary, Admission and Job Placement. Directorate of Medical Teaching of the Ministry of Public Health.

Dr. Roberto Alvarez Sinte. Medical Specialist of 1st and 2nd degree in General Integral Medicine. Master of Science in Medical Education. Assistant Professor. National Methodologist of the career of Medicine. Directorate of Medical Teaching of the Ministry of Public Health.

Dr. Alejandra Keeling Felip: Medical Graduate. First and Second Degree Specialist in General Comprehensive Medicine. Master in Integral Care of the Child. Assistant Professor. Methodologist of teaching staff. Directorate of Medical Teaching of the Ministry of Public Health.

MSc. Alina Leiva Rojas: Bachelor in Health Technology, Clinical Laboratory profile. Master of Science. Assistant Professor. Associate Researcher. Senior Health Specialist. Directorate of Medical Teaching of the Ministry of Public Health.

Dr. Tamara Portelles Morales: Graduate in Stomatology. Master of Science. Assistant Professor. Senior Specialist in Health. Directorate of Medical Teaching of the Ministry of Public Health.

Dr. Ana Beatriz Moye López: Medical Degree. First Specialist in General Comprehensive Medicine. Instructor Professor. Higher Specialization in Health. Directorate of Medical Teaching of the Ministry of Public Health.

MSc. Ariel García **Sá**nchez: Graduate in Cybernetics-Mathematics. Master of Science in Medical Informatics. Specialist Health Advisor. Department of Secretary, Admission and Job Placement. Directorate of Medical Teaching of the Ministry of Public Health.

Lic. Fidel Robinson Jay. Licentiate in Education. Assistant Professor and Researcher. Specialist in Marxism-Leninism. Master in Education Sciences. University of Medical Sciences Guantánamo. Guantánamo. Cuba.

Danay Ramos Duharte. B.A. in Education. Assistant Professor and Researcher.

Specialist in History and Marxism-Leninism. Master in Educational Sciences. University of Guantánamo. Cuba.

Dr. Delia Sotomayor Oliva. Doctor of Medicine. Assistant Professor. Specialist I° MGI. Academic Vice Rector, University of Medical Sciences, Guantanamo. Cuba.

Dr. Marylú Torres Batista. Medical graduate, 2nd degree specialist in Histology, assistant professor, Master in Medical Education. Coordinator of the territorial commission of the EIP. University of Medical Sciences of Holguin.

Dr. Mirna González Sánchez. Medical graduate, second degree specialist in General Comprehensive Medicine, assistant professor, master's degree in Infectious Diseases, Director of Professional Training. Member of the territorial commission of the EIP. University of Medical Sciences of Holguin.

Dr. Emilio Bartolo Serra Hernández. Medical graduate, 2nd degree specialist in General Comprehensive Medicine and in Health Administration, assistant professor, master's degree in Satisfactory Longevity, researcher, Postgraduate Director. Member of the territorial commission of the EIP. University of Medical Sciences of Holguin.

Lic. Dunia Escalona Sarmiento. Graduate of Bachelor's Degree in Nursing, assistant professor, master's degree in Medical Education, Methodologist of the Directorate of Professional Training. Member of the territorial commission of the EIP. University of Medical Sciences of Holguin.

Felix Yunior Rojas Torres. Graduate of Bachelor's Degree in Nursing, assistant professor, Head of the Methodological Teaching Department of Health Technologies, Member of the territorial commission of the EIP and Representative of the ETP. University of Medical Sciences of Holguin.

Néstor González Bahr. Graduate in health administration and economics, Head of the Human Capital Department of the Health Directorate of Holguín Province. University of Medical Sciences of Holguín.

Lic. María Cristina Núñez Martínez: Graduate of Dispensary Pharmacy and Education. Specialty in Biology. Master's Degree in Education. Assistant Professor. Associate Researcher. University of Medical Sciences of Cienfuegos.

Lizgrace Llano Arana. Lic: Graduate in Education. Major in Biology. Master in Medical Education. Head of the Methodological Teaching Department of the FCMC. Assistant Professor. University of Medical Sciences of Cienfuegos.

Addys Teresita Table Rodriguez: Graduate in Education. Specialty in Chemistry. Master in Education. Head of the Department of Basic Subjects and General Education of the FCMC. Assistant Professor. University of Medical Sciences of Cienfuegos.

Dr. Aristides L. García Herrera. Graduate in Medicine. 2nd Degree Specialist in Angiology and Vascular Surgery. Doctor in Medical Sciences Professor and Titular Researcher. Rector of the University of Medical Sciences of Matanzas.

MS c. M a videy Su arez Mer ino. Bachelor of Science in Nursing. Master of Science. Assistant Professor and Researcher. University of Medical Sciences of Matanzas.
Arialys Hernández Nariño. Industrial Engineer. PhD in Technical Sciences. Professor and Researcher. Director of Science and Technological Innovation of the University of Medical Sciences of Matanzas.

Chapter 1

T e o r i c, c onc e ptua l a nd me th olog i c b a se s

The demands of the new millennium, the situation and conditions of the country, the ever-growing needs of the population, the dizzying and constant development of science, technology and technology, cause changes in various social spheres, including health, and in order to assimilate these challenges it is necessary to train personnel to meet these expectations. This requires a comprehensive professional training for competence and job performance. Able to float above their time and successfully face the continuous changes of social development.

Cuban Higher Medical Education after the revolutionary triumph has been consistent with this thinking, which has resulted in the progressive improvement of the different training plans for professionals in the sector, with the aim of achieving a continuous improvement in the level of health of the population as a result of the optimization of the services provided with equity, as well as the increase in the effectiveness of professional skills.

"Wherever the part of the medicine is expensive, it also affects humans. "

Hippocrates

To train professionals of the highest quality is to give them all the humanism possible, the highest ethical and moral values, and the broadest sense of belonging to the welfare of the Cuban family and respect for life. Health professionals grown in the unconditionality before the task given by the people, are formed when they are educated, fight and participate actively and in an interprofessional way, of the functioning of each teaching and assistance scenario in our country.

The Cuban Health System is unique and the institutions belonging to it work as a whole, where the Medical University is an essential component of the process. Among books, patients and dreams, the active life of the students of Medical Sciences goes by: a lot of knowledge to learn, diverse functions to perform, but proud and ready to participate in any task. Our context is marked by personal and family dedication and the effort of the Cuban State to prepare highly qualified professionals capable of sustaining and improving the country's health indexes.

According to the bases of the Epistemology of Medical Education Sciences for the year 2015, the Projections of Public Health in Cuba, have been tinged by different changes, from which stands out as a priority, "The strategy **to** strengthen Primary Health

Care and the transfer **of** technology to **this** level **of** care, together with the adaptation **of the** objectives and functions **of** the Ministry of Health ( ), will consolidate the clinic as a leading institution in the National Health **System**").

These actions will contribute to achieving the objectives of reducing mortality and morbidity from non-communicable diseases and other health damages, which are the main causes of illness and death in the Cuban population, being declared, among the fundamental purposes, to significantly reduce out-of-hospital mortality in serious situations such as: ischemic heart disease and its most severe form of presentation, acute myocardial infarction, cerebrovascular disease, bronchial asthma, accidents and aggressions, developing at the same time, actions that allow to successfully face the attention demanded by the aging of the Cuban population.

Within the process of health care in Cuba, the importance that technological applications are acquiring in the prognosis and treatment of many diseases stands out, giving new meaning to the epistemes that underlie and offer internal logical coherence to the Health Sciences and Medical Sciences, as well as their expression in the processes of training and interprofessional development, Therefore, it is also inserted as a consubstantial element with Medical Education as a science, in such a way that any foundation that is incorporated, any area that is updated within medicine and health, is immediately transposed as a support for the contents and organizational forms of medical education.

Epistemology has established itself as an area of development of the sciences by being conceived as.... "theory of knowledge and identified as gnoseology, offering the possibility of knowing the means and technologies of access to knowledge, its nature, scope and transfer of knowledge", or as philosophy of science, in that it sees it as the branch that sustains, validates and criticizes science in the process of construction and continuous reconstruction.

In this sense, from the epistemological basis of the Medical and Health Sciences, in their relationship with their object of study, the strong impact of new knowledge, the access to knowledge from the development of technologies, the ever-increasing demands of society regarding health problems and the quality of life of the population and the development of sciences in general, which currently move from more holistic, multifactorial and transdisciplinary positions, which causes new and substantial questions in epistemological thinking, should be carefully considered.

In view of the above, it is pertinent to mention that with the revolutionary triumph in

1959, the transformations for the benefit of improving the life of man, mainly in education and health, immediately became the rights of the people as an objective of the Revolution. Thus, the socio-medical paradigm began conceptually, forming a professional model with a broad profile, oriented to the care of healthy people through promotion, prevention and rehabilitation actions and where learning was focused on the main health problems of the population, with great challenges still remaining for the current generations.

The National Education System in Cuba is based on a set of principles, among which the Study and Work Principle stands out. The combination of study and work has deep roots in José Martí's conceptions on education, who summarized the most progressive of the Cuban pedagogical ideology when he postulated the need to erase the existing divorce between theory and practice, study and work, intellectual work and manual labor, and advocates the fusion of these activities in the educational work of the school.

There are also norms for the teaching organization with the work-study approach, defined as the ordered set of different academic and formative elements that regulate the students' transit through higher education, fulfilling the expected social task.

The Cuban Medical University faces the current challenge on solid foundations, by political will and decision of the state and the National Health System (SNS) whose institutions are in charge of achieving equity in health and prioritizing the necessary resources in effective interventions that privilege health promotion and prevention actions.

For these reasons, it has a well-defined social mission that is expressed in the training of Physicians, Stomatologists, Graduates in Nursing and Health Technologies required by society, professionals at a higher level where the modes of action are developed in a conscious manner and on a scientific basis, in the institutions of higher education to guarantee the interprofessional and multiprofessional preparation of university students, with a solid scientific-technical, humanistic training and high ideological, political, ethical and aesthetic values, in order to achieve revolutionary, educated, competent, independent and creative professionals, so that they can perform successfully in the various sectors of society in general.

For this reason, a group of **theoretical and methodological actions** is being developed to help improve the quality of teaching and perfect the interprofessional training process through intracurricular and extracurricular components from the time of entry into the Medical Sciences careers with a systemic, participatory approach, among and for the professionals and other workers of the SNS. Upon graduating and joining any of the three levels of health care, they continue their comprehensive training through postgraduate studies for the improvement of all professionals in the system.

When analyzing that professional competencies are the qualities of a person who performs the specific work of a profession or trade with relevant capacity to rationally fulfill its objectives, which is manifested in performing tasks with great attention, accuracy and speed, interprofessional competencies could be valued as the qualities of a person who performs the specific work of his profession with great capacity, who achieves interaction with people from other professions to achieve great attention, accuracy and speed in collaborative practice and fulfill common objectives among all. In addition, currently the theoretical, conceptual and methodological bases of the design of the curricula of the Medical Sciences careers are:

Design of careers with a higher level of essentiality and rationality, aimed at consolidating the students' research-labor training through a greater integration of classes, scientific work and labor practices.

Training of general practitioners to work in positions related to the care of individuals, families, population groups and the community, in primary care institutions and other institutions where health services are provided, where the modes of action are determined according to the fulfillment of four basic functions: assistance, teaching, research and administration.

Training of other health professionals with a broad profile, prepared to work in the wide field of technological processes in health, actively as a member of the health team, providing the necessary information for medical action, where the modes of action are determined according to the fulfillment of four basic functions: assistance, teaching, research and administration.

Existence of an integrating main discipline, which from the first years of the career works on the object of the profession at elementary levels and which, as it goes through the different cycles, contributes to the development of professional skills, to which other curricular axes are integrated, such as humanistic, communication, medical and social ethics, environmentalism, languages, medical informatics and research, among others.

Training of the modes of action that characterize this professional in the real scenarios where the services are provided, taking advantage of all the care resources available in terms of teaching and research, based on teaching-care-research integration.

Design of teaching strategies that combine information and communication technologies with practical teaching in training scenarios. The main form of teaching organization is on-the-job education, also using different forms of group activities and independent work that guarantee active learning of the students.

Integration of the curricular axes both horizontally (intra-cycle or academic year) and vertically (trans-cycle), so that the contents of the basic sciences and the subjects of professional practice are addressed throughout the career.

Educational model with a level of flexibility and decentralization that allows the training centers the necessary diversity, based on the specific conditions of each one of them and the territories where they are located.

The need to have teaching staff sufficiently prepared to direct a truly developmental teaching-learning process, in order to enhance students' learning, taking as a starting point the organization of their individual activity depending on their own characteristics, experiences and individual potential, on the one hand, and the system of influences that affect them depending on the context and the student group, on the other.

Preparation and accreditation of the different teaching scenarios where the training processes are developed, as well as the teaching media system to be used by students and teachers.

A comprehensive system of evaluation and control of the teaching process and its actors is required, so that corrective action can be taken as soon as difficulties of any kind are detected.

Teaching process with emphasis on learning, with the students playing a leading role and a change in the role of teachers, who assume a p ara grammatic function as a professional model to be reproduced and a function of organizer and facilitator of this process, where the student must progressively acquire the capacity to learn by himself/herself permanently, throughout his/her professional life, as well as to access and critically select the available scientific information.

Therefore, the theoretical, conceptual and methodological bases of Interprofessional Health Education (IPE) applied at the undergraduate level can be defined as follows:

The training of health professionals with a broad profile to form **collaborative** health work **teams.**

A flexible curriculum for all Medical Science majors (Core, Proprietary, Elective/Elective).

Presence of Basic Specific subjects common to all students of Medical Sciences, with an **integrated** and transdisciplinary **approach**.

Presence of **common and interprofessional curricular axes** throughout the study plan of the different Medical Science careers.

Design of an Integrating Main Discipline, where Education at Work is reflected in real training scenarios, where students from the different careers of Medical Sciences interact as working **teams**, fulfilling individually the skills of each profession.

Existence of Work Education modalities that favor Collaborative Health Practice (Ambulatory Care, Medical On-Call, On-Call Delivery, Ward Visit, Clinical-Radiological Meeting, Clinical-Epidemiological Meeting, Case Presentation, among others).

Presence of the Pre-Professional Practice strengthening teamwork and **the** collaborative and collaborative practices (**PPP**).

Presence of extracurricular activities during the career:

Elective course on "Prevention and Health Promotion"
Cardiopulmonary Resuscitation Course (**CP**)
Elective Course in Natural and Traditional Medicine (MN T)
Elective course on "Environmental Education".
Emergency and Medical Emergencies Course
Community Antivector Program

To all of the above, we must add the inclusion of new terms of Interprofessional Health Education (IPE), from the curricular designs, extracurricular activities, the specialized preparation of the faculty, as well as the strengthening of permanent and continuing education of health professionals and the increase of research and scientific results, all with an interprofessional approach and associated for an interprofessional reading that must be assumed and taught:

Collaborative practice is working collaboratively across professions and/or between organizations with individuals, families, groups and communities.

Formative assessment contributes to student learning through self-assessment of student progress and improvement planning.

Interdisciplinary care is sometimes used as an alternative to interprofessional care or to refer to care provided between different branches of the same profession, usually in medicine.

Interdisciplinary research usually refers to systematic research conducted in collaboration between members of different academic fields.

Interprofessional care is a collaborative response to the needs of individuals, families, groups and communities by members of two or more professions.

Interprofessional education occurs when students or members of two or more professions do or do not learn with, from and about each other to improve collaboration and quality of care.

Interprofessional learning occurs between students or members of two or more professions to improve knowledge and skills in interprofessional education or informally in educational or practice contexts.

Interprofessional practice is the collaboration in practice between students or members of two or more professions, whether or not they are working at the same time.

Interprofessional teamwork involves members of two or more professions, whether or not they have complementary skills to maintain a collaborative practice towards common objectives.

An interprofessional team is a group of students or members of two or more professions, whether or not they study or work in different settings but fulfill the same social role.

Interprofessional research refers both to systematic research in interprofessional education and to interprofessional practice and/or conduct.

Multidisciplinary education is sometimes used alternatively with multiprofessional education (see below), but can also refer to education between branches of the same profession or between academic disciplines.

Multi-professional education occurs when different professions learn side by side for whatever reason.

Undergraduate courses with an interprofessional focus are programs that lead to satisfactory results in obtaining professional qualifications.

Postgraduate courses with an interprofessional focus are programs undertaken after professional qualification to advance knowledge and skills.

Com p art ed or **interprof** essional learning is a generic term used loosely when groups of professionals do or do not learn together.

Summative evaluation is an assessment of the shared or interprofessional learning that has taken place and that counts towards the qualification.

It is also interesting to raise the following questions related to the topic under study, such as: what is interprofessional education, what is the current situation of this educational trend, both worldwide and nationally? When these issues are sufficiently addressed, the objective will have been achieved, which is to identify interprofessional education as an educational trend that has taken off worldwide.

According to WHO, the widespread adoption of an interprofessional education model is an urgent need[2] .

PAHO/WHO developed a regional strategy on human resources for health within the framework of the Global Strategy **on Human Resources** for Health: Health

Workforce 2030. Resolution WHA69.19, adopted at the 69th[a] World Health Assembly in 2016. Interprofessional education is positioning itself in recent years as an essential tool for controlling medical errors, reducing costs and, ultimately, improving the experience of patients and their healthcare.

For Juanjo Beunza, IPE is "the discipline of study and practice related to teamwork where professionals from different fields, for example: nursing, pharmacy, medicine, physiotherapy, etc., interact with each other to provide better patient care"[3] .

Until today, no practical text on interprofessional education in healthcare in Spanish-and/or Portuguese-speaking country settings was available. The Handbook **of** Interprofessional Healthcare Education (**Elsevier** 2018) provides an answer to this need[3] . It is aimed at individuals and institutions that wish to design and implement interprofessional education programs in university settings, or in clinical settings. Dr. Juanjo Beunza, editor of the book, gave an update on IPE and its influence on the present and future of healthcare, in an interview that complemented the II Jornada Nacional de Educación Interprofesional: "Promoting healthcare collaboration", organized by the Universidad Europea de Madrid.

The content of his answers can be assumed to describe the current state of this educational trend in the world. He expressed that the United Kingdom and Canada are probably the two reference countries in both interprofessional education and collaborative practice. Japan is also, especially for the adaptation of its healthcare system to what is probably the oldest population in the world. Quite a model, and a challenge, for all of us[4] .

He points out that the United Kingdom, Canada, Japan, Sweden, etc. have been implementing Interprofessional Education programs for more than 15 years, and their use is widespread in health faculties. In some of these countries it is in fact mandatory. In the USA they have only been in place for a few years, but they have made a great economic effort to ensure that implementation is rapid and widespread.

In Spanish and Portuguese-speaking countries, there have been isolated actions in universities and hospitals for some years now, but there are very few integrated and systematic programs.

However, the push being made by the Pan American Health Organization (PAHO/WHO) is gigantic. As of today, there are more than 14 countries in Latin America, which through their ministries of health have already proposed a national plan for the development of Interprofessional Education, linked to Universal Health Access (Agenda for Sustainable Development 2030). In fact, PAHO has issued

Resolution CSP29.R15 of September 2017 where it specifies the use of Interprofessional Education. It is a time of great explosion in the design and implementation of program s[4] .

He concludes by saying that with a view to the future, the ideal healthcare scenario, including EIP, would be a matrix healthcare system based on the patient at home and in the community, where all professionals have simple and easy tools for communication and interaction among themselves, with great implementation of the "internet of things" in homes and technological tools so that the patient can easily contact his or her health professional of reference, and through him or her, with all the others[4] .

During a meeting held in Bogota, Colombia, during December 7-9, 2016, under the theme: "Interprofessional education in health care: improving human resources capacity to achieve universal health"[5] , its main results were collected in a detailed report and stakeholders are updated on the subject in our geographical area.

On this stage Dr. John Gilbert, Professor Emeritus, University of British Columbia, Adjunct Professor, Dalhousie University; Founding President, Canadian Interprofessional Health Collaborative (CIHC) began his presentation by holding a smart phone in his hand and saying it was the best tool he has ever known for teaching. He said that technology has changed in important ways, and the future of medical education depends on it.

Dr. Gilbert's position during more than 50 years of teaching has changed markedly. However, his role continues to guide the intellect of young people who are eager to learn that there are places on the path of learning worth visiting. It is important to recognize that, these days, books are not really the primary source of information for our students. Books that once rested on shelves in a very large building can now be retrieved electronically for common learning, constituting what is the field of common or distributed learning.

Traditional education maintained the text-classroom-workplace form. The purpose of going to class was to get an education and then continue to the workplace to learn how to do the job. Now technology gives education the ability to distribute learning across that continuum, taking us to a very different place.

Chapter 2

The amount of the loan is deducted.

Distributed learning is now text-computer-online/network-connection-audioconferencing-video conferencing-classroom-workplace. The ability to teach by teleconference or videoconference brought us back to the classroom, but the classroom is no longer here, the classroom is out there somewhere. Some taxonomies of learning include the use of technology and didactic support. Smartphones are now a learning tool for students and a tool for physicians to reach rural communities.

"Education is not filling a pot, it is lighting a fire"[5] . Distributed learning allows us to light the fire in many different ways besides reading a book. In this same context, Tobar Almonacid, representative of the Faculty of Medicine of the University of Chile at this meeting, stated that "university accreditation regulates various aspects of the training of health professionals, but does not incorporate IPE"[5] . In Cuba, the National Accreditation Board (JAN) could play an important role for universities to assume and implement this new paradigm or educational trend.

For Silva and collaborators, the challenge now lies in giving continuity to what has been programmed on EIP in our region or geographic area. And we already have results.

The Regional Interprofessional Education Network of the Americas (REIP)[7] , under the coordination of Argentina, Brazil and Chile, presented its candidacy to become a member of the World Coordinating Committee of All Together Better Health (WCC-ATBH), which is an organization made up of regional networks focused on interprofessional health education and practices and includes representatives from all over the world, which can strengthen, above all, the exchange of experiences on IPE in the Region of the Americas.

Brazil is making progress in this area with proposals to incorporate these topics in the curricula of undergraduate health careers and in the formulation of proposals for teacher qualification, as has been done in Bolivia, Cuba, Chile, Honduras and Peru. In Argentina and Guyana, proposals for research in this area are already being discussed. Guatemala, Nicaragua, Panama and Venezuela have presented strategies for the qualification of health professionals, using the theoretical and methodological bases of IPE.

Some countries have already proposed the creation of national IPE networks, such as the Dominican Republic and Suriname, while others, such as Paraguay, Uruguay,

Colombia and Costa Rica, are recognizing the insertion of the topic in the national reality by conducting studies.

The hope now is that countries can in fact, in cooperation with PAHO/WHO, implement IPE as a potential approach to strengthening health systems, because in today's global context it is not enough for health professionals to be professionals, they must also be interprofessionals[6] .

According to Díaz Quiñones, "Cuban higher medical education has potentialities that are expressed in its main strengths, which distinguish it from other medical training systems and place it in a privileged position worldwide, such as: the principle of on-the-job education throughout the entire career, which allows a constant relationship with the profession's object of work, the main modes of action and the different health problems to be faced in its future performance in different scenarios that enhance the relationship between theory and practice and university and society".

Undoubtedly, this has made possible the development that can be seen today in the country's human resources and will undoubtedly facilitate the successful implementation of the precepts and practices of IPE in the context of medical science teaching institutions in the country.

Postgraduate studies as a development pathway for Interprofessional Health Education

Interprofessional Education (IPE) in Health refers to the preparation achieved as a result of the whole system of educational actions, whether pedagogical or didactic, which through interactive learning favor the development and comprehensive collaborative success in the performance of health professions and professionals. In this sense, we assume the category of Interprofessional Education in its two dimensions (professional and for life), from which we try to reestablish the essential connection between school and life (first law of Pedagogy), study and work, theory and practice, training and social performance as it is directed to the improvement of collaboration between the different profiles of health and social care in patient care and problem solving in this complex field.

Higher Education in Health, as responsible for the preparation of human capital through the institutions in charge of the training and development of its professionals, is responsible for the improvement of the educational dynamics where they reach a high scientific-technical qualification and solidity in the socio-humanistic development that puts them in capacity of a high level in the performance of their professional model, with coherence profession-mode of action that favors the maximum quality in their service with satisfaction of the population, tasks for which postgraduate education offers ample possibilities to achieve them.

Postgraduate education is one of the main directions of work and the highest level of the system of Higher Education in Cuba, aimed at promoting the continuing education of university graduates.

The Postgraduate Education Regulation of the Ministry of Higher Education, which sets out the main directions of Higher Education in Cuba, is an example of the importance given by the Cuban state to this activity as the highest level of this subsystem, aimed at promoting the continuing education of university graduates, from which their improvement is derived, in correspondence with the development of science, technique, technology and the fundamental contents of the general comprehensive culture required by professionals for a competent performance.

The importance of graduate education is based on the historical evidence of the centrality of education, research and collective learning in development processes; and the need for lifelong education, supported by self-management of learning and socialization in the construction of knowledge.

For this reason, an integral system of Postgraduate Education was established to respond to the constant improvement of the graduate, from the time he/she graduates until he/she stops working as a professional. To this end, Postgraduate Education was divided into two main areas, one leading to scientific degrees (Scientific Degrees System) and the other aimed at guaranteeing the necessary cyclical improvement of all Higher Education graduates (Professional Improvement System).

Professional Advancement, unlike the system of scientific degrees, is aimed at all graduates, since at any given moment it is possible for any of them to improve their knowledge or skills to improve the work they perform or to cover new functions. It became necessary to organize and develop all these concepts according to the country's needs. In Cuba, there are few antecedents of Postgraduate Education reflected fundamentally by the strong individual improvement of professionals in general.

The process of improvement for professionals is closely linked to a branch of pedagogy in Cuba, the pedagogy of Technical and Vocational Education (TVE), which studies the essence, regularities and trends of educational phenomena, as consciously structured processes, has its specific principles resulting from the particularities of its object of study.

The process of Technical and Vocational Education (TVE) is identified as a continuous process, it has its own characteristics that make it similar to other educational processes, it is a social, dia lectic, systemic and systematic, flexible and creative, polyvalent, organized, theoretical-practical, investigative, contradictory, coherent, labor education, productive and investigative process. According to the authors, all these characteristics assume a particular nuance that, although similar to other processes, also differentiate it, which serves as a basis for the fundamentals related to the improvement of health professionals.

This process of improvement calls for a developmental education in line with the continuous development of science, technique and technology (STS), which is the foundation on which the improvement of health professionals is based.

Assuming the ideas of Julia Añorga (1995), who sees professional development as an education that contributes to form men of science with certain values, since not only knowledge is transmitted and skills are developed, but also man's behavior is enriched to identify, analyze and solve his own problems, with decision making and interacting with the environment and with Society. From its theoretical position, the orientation of the process of improvement is recognized, but it does not reveal the dialectical relationships that allow an understanding of the dynamics of the processes inherent to professional improvement, as a process that has to contemplate new perspectives of development according to the context where it is developed.

The process of development of Interprofessional Education at the postgraduate level can be beneficial for the incorporation of useful knowledge of the sciences to the way of professional performance, which contribute to the elevation of scientific culture, as well as to the increase of professional and life competences. This integration becomes possible in the graduate program when three essential concepts for the permanent development of the professional are articulated: the pertinence of the training actions, the transcendence of the teaching management in the graduate program and the impact of its contextualized performance, both in those who provide and in those who receive the services.

Relevance, which implies the adequacy of the process in responding to the socio-professional demands by making the necessary changes at the right time, depending on the context in which it is developed.

Transcendence, in that it implies a greater scope, so that in the process of developing interprofessional education, while acquiring new knowledge, developing skills and incorporating and strengthening values, higher levels of integral quality are achieved, preparing them for the changes that are required.

The impact, which reflects the result left by the training in the context in which the professional must work and in which, as a value

The added value of the program has an impact on the achievement of adequate indicators of satisfaction in the individual, the family and the community.

Taking into consideration the idea that it is imperative to transform the traditional views, criteria and values inherited from higher medical education, the postgraduate program constitutes an ideal process for the development of the interprofessional education that is intended in health, starting from the point that the graduates of the various profiles already have experiential, professional and social experiences, personal, intellectual, motivational, valuational and attitudinal resources in function of a real know-how to act facing the complexity of today's health problems with satisfactory results as well as defined interests, necessary precedents for the precision of their learning needs, of procedural and attitudinal development in the health service and for the axiological evaluation of the results of the same.

These transformations should be achieved as a result of the implementation of strategies and/or systems of actions (pedagogical, didactic, methodological or improvement) designed with implementation schedules, measurement criteria and quality indicators, as well as improvement plans that serve to validate the effectiveness of the changes made in the sustainable development of human capital. Hence the importance of scientific educational research in health.

Fundamementsofinterprofessionaleducationinthepregr aphism

For the execution of any educational process at present, it is required the establishment of the theoretical foundations on which the actions planned for its achievement will be developed, corroborating the value of scientific research. From this principle, the authors were able to identify the social, economic and cultural influences of the specific historical context of our country in which interprofessional education will be developed as the educational work demanded with the human capital in Health.

The relationship between education and society, seen as the objective basis of the educational process in health to achieve the integration of its graduates to the social context, as well as the influence of education in the construction of health as a value of society, require that, in the design of educational actions and their execution, in our case the graduate program, the set of theoretical foundations that give coherence to the educational theory be taken into account.

Interprofessional education, as an educational process of change in health professionals, is developed in a certain social context that delineates economic foundations, sociological points of view, systems of philosophical ideas, didactic pedagogical conceptions, legal frameworks, psychological requirements, health fundamentals, so it is necessary to analyze the foundations that will support the critical path to follow in the solution of the problem being studied in this educational process.

The research conducted by a group of experts led by the University of Medical Sciences of Guantanamo allows us to situate the following systems of ideas as theoretical foundations of postgraduate education as a way for the development of Interprofessional Health Education:

PHILOSOPHICS

There is a need for comprehensive conceptual and lubricity systems that provide support for the

health service

Socio-humanist thought: the welfare of man as the center of social activity.

The solution of ethical conflicts in the health service oriented to increase the quality of life.

Health thinking: health as a process of social construction of human wellbeing.

Those principles and values and ethics that are the basis of true professional attitudes and correct interprofessional relationships that favor teamwork must be identified and socialized.

EC ONOMICS

Collaborative economy in healthcare is imperative

The collaborative health economy.

Social responsibility with the financing and improvement of health services.

Cost savings in health care.

Health cost-benefit ratio.

SOCIOLOGICAL

Better attention to the increased complexity of social health problems is needed.

Health as a social value.

The social political responsibility of the States and their health systems with the life and well-being of their citizens.

Social intersectoriality in the solution of health problems.

PEDAGOGICAL

There is a need to improve professional training in the health sector

The link between school and social life.

The dialectics of the cognitive process.

The value of pedagogy in the design and evaluation of training processes for health professionals.

The systemic conception in health professional preparation.

DIDÁ CTIC **OS**

Improvements in health teaching and learning processes are demanded.

Recognition of the role of Didactics in the design and evaluation of learning.

Value of task sequences in preparation and self-development.

Learning, its environments and styles.

The process of teaching to learn.

Interactivity in learning

PSYCHOLOGICALS

The development of the health professional's personality through activity and communication.

The role of the dialogical positions of the actors.

The purpose of social mediation between providers and recipients of health care.

Consistency is demanded between what health professionals think and what patients think and feel.

LEGA **LES**

The right to quality health care is enshrined in the Constitution and the national laws that make it a reality.

The struggle for the realization of the right to health for all.

Legislative advances that commit the State to the improvement of health professionals to better serve its population.

Raising the level of university graduates is endorsed by legislation

SA LUBRISTA **S**

Increased quality in health systems and services is required.

Interprofessional collaboration in the care of people.

Collaborative practice in health care.

Equity instead of hierarchization of knowledge

Leadership according to the health problem to be solved.

Integrality in health care.

Valuing the importance of the proper interweaving of the science system with health care practice, as well as with social innovation in the health sector, the need to develop aspects that address the political, social and ethical reflection of science and technology in this sector is reaffirmed. Therefore, the development of reflective thinking on interprofessionalism, of argumentative foundations for collaborative practice and of individual and group creativity are immediate goals to be achieved in graduate education by health professionals.

The postgraduate training and development of human resources in the health sector should be strengthened with the implementation of the tools of Pedagogy and Didactics as guiding sciences of all educational processes, the study from the cosmovisional character of Philosophy, Psychology for its decisive incidence in the training and management of professionals, of the clear understanding of the political, social and ethical conditions of the society in general and of the health activity in particular and with a solid base in the effective use of the Information and Communication Technologies through teaching activities focused on the self-management of knowledge, which favor the achievement of the efficient postgraduate improvement of the health professionals.

The positive results and favorable impacts on the training processes of health professionals in Cuba are the result of the recognized work of Higher Education in Health through its Universities of Medical Sciences (UCM), which have in their teaching staffs prestigious professors who have accumulated valuable training experiences, as a result of different teaching and academic work and training in national and international universities of recognized expertise in the area in which they work.

The multifactorial origin of health-disease problems generates, for their successful management, the need for interprofessional collaboration.

Complementarity and collaboration provide greater prospects for success in healthcare practice when healthcare providers are working collaboratively.

Common objectives are sought that favor the analysis and solution of any problem that may arise in the health care of individuals, groups and society.

From this point of view, it is considered that Interprofessional Education contributes to the development of the competences of their professional profile, which are fundamental in the performance of multidisciplinary teams and in collaborative practice, such as interpersonal communication, authority management and decision making, as well as the execution of roles: definition, design and defense of criteria, projects and systems of related actions.

Interprofessional Education also seeks to develop those competencies that have been shown to be fundamental for life, in particular socio-humanistic competencies, those linked to a civic and democratic culture, the confrontation and prevention of social ills, as well as the preservation and care of the environment.

In order to achieve the aforementioned, strategic pedagogical thinking must be its essential theoretical tool, aimed at the continuous increase of effectiveness in the fundamental dimensions of the training process: teaching-education, ideological policy, moral ethics, civic-social, scientific-research and labor extension.

Interprofessional research as a way to solve health issues

The revealing technological and scientific advances that are currently recognized in this century imply an integrative learning in professionals, as they are responsible for the solution of the problems faced by mankind through decision making that favors coherent actions in the face of different problematic situations. The accelerated technological development achieved in health services implies a high level of preparation of its professionals.

The problems identified in the work context and the strategies of the National Health System are elements that favor the need for an obligatory space to put into practice research skills in health professionals, thus becoming contents of improvement in correspondence to the current technological development.

In this context, the Medical University has carried out a series of transformations in the design of its undergraduate and graduate curricula with an interdisciplinary and interprofessional approach, aimed at developing autonomous and integrative learning, strengthening the humanistic training of graduates and developing research skills, even though these interprofessional work teams have a great impact on society due to the benefits they bring to the National Health System, they must provide services to the population with a collaborative approach and sufficient comprehensive preparation according to the demands of society in order to contribute to the sustainable development of the country.

Nowadays, interprofessional work teams must be prepared to face new technologies and develop technological processes with quality. They must also preserve the environment by using existing conventional and advanced methods.

Therefore, it is necessary to pay direct attention to these professionals through

Postgraduate Education, which emerged in Cuba as a consequence of the impetuous development of the productive forces, of the development of Education in general and of Higher Education in particular, in the years following the triumph of the Revolution, and constitutes the highest level within the National Education System.

From this perspective, the competitiveness of university health institutions should be guaranteed, according to learning needs, as well as the planning and execution of training activities in any of its modalities, in order to aspire that health professionals are trained professionals of excellence, linked to the management of biomedical technologies, with the capacity to perform interprofessional and integrative assistance functions, of promotion, prevention, treatment and rehabilitation of health to healthy and/or sick people, in a reciprocal relationship with their natural and social environment, which is based on human health needs and their satisfaction, as well as administrative, teaching and research functions, with the purpose of transforming health services and medical care at different levels.

It is understood then that in order to plan and carry out a process of improvement that guarantees the successful execution of professional performance, it is necessary to inquire about the level of knowledge and the development of research skills, providing flexible and viable solutions to the problems detected in the technological practice. Today it is emphasized that there is no true higher education without explicit and implicit research activity, which is part of the teaching-learning process and has a great value in professional training.

It is a contextualized process; research cannot be seen in isolation, but inserted in global and work-related problems; it must be conceived in a direct relationship with the problems that society is experiencing. Research is done to transform reality and thus contribute to human development and therefore to improve the quality of life, so that research is a very valuable means to achieve any transformation in the professional field.

Professionals in the Medical Sciences receive in the undergraduate program the Discipline of Informatics and Research, which is responsible for providing the knowledge, skills and values for research that will allow future professionals to successfully face research tasks. These skills are aimed at four fundamental aspects, the search and management of scientific information, the development of scientific language, the use of biostatistics and computing in research tasks and the mastery of the different categories of the Methodology of Scientific Research, so that they can apply the scientific method to the problems that arise in the performance of their functions for the improvement of the processes in which they participate and assume the transformations with responsibility, motivation and creativity according to their own professional and human interests.

The mastery of Research Methodology, the permanent updating of the advances in science and technology, in addition to the results of developmental learning, will achieve professional and human improvement in postgraduate training, which is subject to the permanent and continuous professional improvement of each professional to enable him/her to meet the individual and social needs of the training process for the health care of the Cuban population, where the scientific basis generates different analyses.

From the analysis of the theory of Advanced Education, one can glimpse greater aspirations in health professionals, which are manifested in what Dr. Añorga recognizes as professional and human **improvement**, which from its interpretation and contextualization are manifested in the intellectual, physical and spiritual development, knowing their problems, aspirations, motivations, in the professional and personal aspects, in order to contribute to the solution of the problems corresponding to their social, labor and family context, turning the problems detected into contents of different activities of improvement in correspondence to the technological development reached in the National Health System, through an intellectual and scientific production with quality.

The participatory and reflective nature of these professionals in the different forms of professional development, make them incorporate what they have learned to their daily performance, seeking solutions to the problems detected, applying the scientific method, and bringing about new concerns to be investigated and scientific expectations to be implemented, which promote the intellectual production of these professionals.

From the point of view of the Medical Education Sciences, today a postgraduate curriculum is required that is nourished by the health problems of the population, by the development of technologies in correspondence with the services and health care, which includes health education and, of course, by the demands of the ever-changing and dynamic society. These relationships offer the Medical Education Sciences logical coherence in the area of permanent and continuous training of health professionals.

The proposed training activities should collect the detected problems and turn them into training contents with an interprofessional approach, expressing the deepening of knowledge through reading and self-preparation of the professionals. The proposed solutions for the development of scientific activity through training should be flexible, feasible and viable for practical implementation in any health context.

It is necessary to obtain revealing results in the scientific-research activity of health professionals, through the increase and development of research skills and intellectual production, participation and presentation of papers in scientific events and the application of these results in the technological process to offer excellent services to the population.

Pedagogical tools with an interprofessional approach for the preparation of the troop

The changes made possible by the Revolution, the impetuous advance of science and technology and their application in medical practice, the social character of health sciences and their focus on aspects that address the health of the community and not only the illness of the individual, have led to the imperative of training, as part of the human resources for health, a competent professional capable of carrying out the social functions demanded of him/her.

The Interprofessional Education (IPE) needs solvent and effective pedagogical tools that will articulate pedagogical processes that contribute to improve the guidelines of Higher Education, as well as the link between study and work, the continuous and quality improvement of teachers, with emphasis on new teachers, scientific research, transfer of knowledge and analysis of their discipline with other disciplines and educational centers, scientific and cultural exchange with other countries in an integrated manner; All of the above will allow the development and potentialities of the faculty to be incorporated into the training process among professionals and for professionals, providing that the educational aspects acquire greater relevance in the teaching decisions about the evaluation of learning with a developmental approach.

Every day the university needs a faculty prepared to train more competent professionals with a broad and interdisciplinary profile and a greater comprehensive training, essential for these times, which allows them to solve the main problems that arise in the different spheres of action and fields of action, and if they are able to socialize with other professionals, to establish collaborative spaces with interprofessional groups and achieve an effective collaborative practice, satisfactory results and new knowledge that enrich the Interprofessional Education in health can be expected.

Therefore, it must be taken into account that academic excellence is characterized by three dimensions: the excellence of human resources, in particular of the faculty and students; the excellence of the material base, both that which is available in the universities and that which is used in the territory; the excellence of the management of university processes; and the excellence of the university processes. [1.]

Therefore, it is pertinent to organize, plan and execute a system of improvement actions directed to teachers (according to teaching category, scientific degree, teaching and/or administrative functions) that will allow them to increase their competencies and integral teaching performance, and influence the quality of the teaching-learning process, which will allow teachers to be updated according to the new transformations and the new educational technologies for the updating of teaching.

At the frontiers of teaching and the primary role of faculty is to evaluate the effectiveness of IPE interventions in comparison to education interventions in which professionals in specific fields learn separately from each other, it is necessary to evaluate that effectiveness in comparison to the need to identify and employ useful pedagogical tools for improvement, which can be derived from:

The use of technologies applied to education (TE) The teaching of learning theories and approaches The implementation of digital tools

In the academic component there is an intellectual space whose object of study is the media and information and communication technologies (ICT) as forms of representation, dissemination and access to knowledge and culture in different educational contexts: non-formal education, basic schooling, distance education and higher education".[2]

The faculty must use Educational Technologies as the basic foundation of Interprofessional Education (IPE), which took place in the United States in the 1950s. In this sense, it has given rise to different approaches or trends that are known as audiovisual teaching, programmed teaching, instructional technology, curriculum design or critical teaching technology.

Educational Technologies provide teachers with the planning and development tools necessary to carry out the teaching and learning processes through technological resources with the aim of improving them to maximize the progress of educational objectives and seek the success of learning in different training environments that can be: face-to-face with technological equipment, blended or online when using mobile technologies (m-learning) and the use of platforms.

It is also necessary to know the aspects that involve the different educational technologies and that in turn make up, in a practical way, components of the pedagogical tools to promote interprofessional education (IPE) aimed at improving collaboration between different types of health professionals in the area of teaching, thus avoiding learning separately from each other and in the absence of an adequate, effective and systematic intervention.

The characteristics of the implementation of Educational Technologies in the teaching and learning processes and their flow of activities in Interprofessional Education (IPE) by the teacher are related to:

The incorporation of proposals to the educational curriculum to work by subjects or in an interdisciplinary way.

The use of educational platforms for content management inside and outside the classroom.

Constant updating.

The versatility of pedagogical proposals. Depending on the content and type of technology, different pedagogical proposals based on constructionism can be made.

Regardless of the processes of evolution of education and its complex theoretical framework, three stages are considered in the evolution of the development of Educational Technologies up to the dawn of the 21st century:

The first stage was conceived as a "learning aid" with the objective of introducing new instruments and procedures in teaching, then in a second stage, according to the approaches of various authors, it was conceived as a "learning aid" in which it was intended to optimize learning.

But the development of the sciences showed that a new era could emerge beyond the classroom where well-designed methodologies could concur and referred to Educational Technologies as a systematic approach to education that forces the entire academic community to interact and that includes a set of procedures or protocols based on scientific knowledge that allow the design and development of educational programs in a systematic and rational way.

The references in various sources agree that Educational Technologies offer a sufficiently coherent and solid body of knowledge on how to organize the variables that affect learning in order to plan instructional environments and processes aimed at achieving educational objectives.

Basic tools

Depending on time and needs, the tools used in the IPE processes vary:

Cloud services: Google Drive, Onedrive and Dropbox.

Messaging and social networks: Skype, WhatsApp, Hangouts, SnapChat, Telegram, Allo, Twitter and email.

Content presentations: Slideshare, Prezi, Padlet, Emaze among others.

Collaborative tools: forums, Blogs, wikis and Webquest.

LMS: Edmodo, Schoology, among others.

Creation tools

The creation tools are associated with programming, where users not only consume information but also create information, content and programs, which is why they are related to programming tools:

Scratch

APP Inventor

At present we can find various learning theories and pedagogical approaches on which IPE bases its theoretical perspectives and which at the same time focus its concepts in the field of elementary tools to develop multidisciplinary processes. These theories are grouped into the following philosophical frameworks: behaviorism, constructivism and constructionism.

C onduc t ism

This theoretical framework was developed in the early 20th century, based on animal learning experiments conducted by Ivan Pavlov, Edward Thorndike, Edward C. Tolman, Clark L. Hull and B.F. Skinner. The teaching of behaviorism has been linked to training, emphasizing animal learning experiments. Since behaviorism consists of the idea of teaching people how to do something with rewards and punishments, it is related to the training of people[12] .

B.F. Skinner wrote extensively about improvements in teaching based on his functional analysis of verbal behavior[1314] , and wrote "The Technology of Teaching",[1516] an attempt to dispel the myths underlying contemporary education and promote his system he called programmed instruction. Ogden Lindsley developed a learning system, called Celeration, which was based on behavioral analysis but differed substantially from the models of Keller and Skinner.

C ons truct iv ism

Constructivism holds that each learner structures his or her knowledge of the world through a unique pattern, connecting each new fact, experience or understanding into a subjectively growing structure that leads the learner to establish rational and meaningful relationships with the world.[17] A person who learns something new incorporates it into his previous experiences and his own mental structures. Each new information is assimilated and deposited in a network of knowledge and experiences that exist previously in the subject, as a result we can say that learning is neither passive nor objective, on the contrary it is a subjective process that each person is constantly modifying in the light of his experiences. Constructivism has the theories of Jean Piaget (1952), Lev Vygotsky (1978), David Ausubel (1963), Jerome Bruner (1960), and even though none of them called themselves constructivists, their ideas and proposals clearly illustrate the ideas of this current.[18]

C ons trucc ion is mo

Constructionism, proposed by Seymour Papert, as a contemporary learning theory arises from Piaget's constructivist theory, emphasizing the value of ICTs as useful tools for developing critical thinking. The basic premise assumes the existence of a natural ability in human beings to learn through experience, and to create mental structures that organize and synthesize the information and experiences of everyday life. Papert focused not on instructional forms of learning but on giving students the opportunity to build. Papert is therefore the pioneer of the theory of computer-assisted learning to develop the creative process in the minds of learners. [19]

Today we have different tools and platforms that we can use, whether for communication between the entire teaching environment, monitoring or even the evaluation of different skills.

The platforms allow us to apply E-learning techniques, to be fulfilled, minimum characteristics are needed, such as:

Networking.

To be delivered to the end user through a computer integrating Internet technology standards.

To broaden the perspective of learning so that it moves a step beyond traditional training paradigms.[21]

If these characteristics are met, we are talking about an interprofessional e-learning platform. These can be structured into two fundamental components:

Free software platforms. They refer to those that are free for all. An example widely used today is Moodle.[22] .

Proprietary software platforms. These are developed and implemented within the educational institution itself.

Other authors are of the opinion that Interprofessional Education (IPE) is a necessary step for health professionals to be prepared for collaborative practice, an indispensable dimension to establish true teamwork and thus respond to the health needs of the population.

It is unavoidable and useful to ask ourselves what methodological tools can be built and used to facilitate the preparation of the teaching staff to face this challenge? In order to achieve its development in Cuba, it is necessary to prepare the teaching staff and provide them with the necessary pedagogical tools to succeed in this activity.

For the World Health Organization, Interprofessional Education (IPE) is "a pedagogical strategy in which members or students of two or more health or social care professions engage in learning with, about and with each other"[1] .

He further adds that IPE "provides students with the ability to share skills and knowledge across professions; allows for better understanding; shared values; and respect for the roles of other health professionals. Its early development, before students begin their internships, builds a core value of working within interprofessional teams"[1] . This basic value referred to here should be the capacity or competence to work in solidarity in teams, thus meeting the health needs of the population.

How teachers teach and the way students learn will not change for at least 5,000 years. Students are expected to remember what teachers have told them or what they have read in order to compile some facts that then become new information.

The existence of actions that act as tools to strengthen the preparation of teaching staffs in Interprofessional Education activities is pertinent. Their design and implementation are two demanding tasks. These challenges or tasks include teachers' interest and prior knowledge about IPE, a culture of valuing shared learning between teachers and students, the possibility of exchanges of experiences, curricular redesign, course scheduling, adequacy of course content, and ministerial and institutional policies to meet the challenge and develop all the necessary logistics, from the central level to the schools. With the intention of proposing some tools as possible solutions, the following suggestions are given:

1. Stimulate and guarantee the didactic-methodological preparation of all teachers, through concrete instructional and demonstrative activities on IPE, to be developed in a planned way in all organizational structures, from the teaching department to the faculty and university level. (The pedagogical tool would be the Pla n de Trabalho Métodolóqico, elaborated as established by the ministerial resolution 02/2018).

2. Train teachers and facilitators on IPE topics so that they are responsible for supporting students in developing competencies for working in an interdisciplinary cooperative team that addresses diverse health situations, building on students' prior learning and identifying the roles of the different team members. Students should also go through a training process before they begin to collaborate with interprofessional groups. (The tool would be professional development).

3. Propose that the requirement of interprofessional education be included in the graduate exit profile, making the incorporation of IPE mandatory in all careers in a standardized manner. (The tool would be the medical career matrix).

4. Propose that regulatory entities and guarantors of the prestige of universities in Cuba, such as the JAN, include in some of its variables, specific quality indicators related to aspects of the EIP. (The tool would be the accreditation process to which careers and universities are periodically submitted).

5. Define professional profiles according to the health needs and expectations of the population, involving curricular revisions and detecting, among other elements, common aspects among professions and among curricula, not only in terms of what should be implemented but also in terms of what already exists and can be generalized. (The tool would be the curriculum of each medical science career).

6. To ensure that the governing bodies or ministries and educational institutions adapt their organization charts and teaching methods to

promote interprofessional education and collaborative teaching practice, through the teaching and learning process (PEA), which is deployed in each career. (The tools in this case would be the courses, internships, modules and subjects that are designed with an EIP approach).

For this purpose, it would be convenient:

Generate **mega-transversal courses** and **internships** with students from two or more health professions, with professors in charge and facilitators, duly trained, to develop contents with EIP projections.

Design, plan and deliver interdisciplinary and **multiprofessional** modules, also with teachers in charge and facilitators, duly trained, to develop contents with EIP projections.

Design, offer and teach within the current flexible curriculum (Plans D), elective and **elective subjects** that meet the needs of the territory and at the same time introduce theoretical and practical contents with an interprofessional approach.

7. These courses, internships, modules, and courses can provide the skills to integrate the knowledge, skills, and values of various health professions and work with disciplines from other careers in real and virtual environments, including different perspectives on how to approach a case or a health problem. .

8. To develop these courses, internships, modules and subjects, teaching methods and learning resources or tools within our reach can be used, such as.

   Problémica teaching, because through its methods (problémica exposition, partial search, heuristic conversation, investigative method) the teaching and learning process is activated and the analysis of health problems is facilitated.

   Simulated teaching, which allows students to relate a clinical case to the basic knowledge acquired, which further develops their professional skills.

   Health teamwork, which forces students to consider others and apply their knowledge to solve health problems in a multidisciplinary and interprofessional manner.

Information and communication technologies (ICT) because, through educational software, computer platforms and even social networks, it is possible to disseminate and manage information quickly and efficiently.

9. Develop transversal competencies in ethics and bioethics with respect to behavior in the face of ethical problems. These competencies will have a major impact on interdisciplinary teamwork and interprofessional collaboration. During this process, it will also be important to gather evidence and create indicators to evaluate the results.

10. Stimulate and facilitate the publication of articles and materials describing the experience gathered in these courses, integrated modules, own subjects, electives, etc., which would illustrate the importance of contributing to the core of knowledge on IPE. (The tools in this case would be pedagogical research, generalization and timely publication of the results achieved).

11. Promote and participate in national and international events on IPE, in which, through programs based on lectures, round tables and workshops coordinated by prestigious experts and researchers from different parts of the world, it is possible to share experiences and at the same time create the possibility of generating new perspectives from multidisciplinary work, synergy between health areas and dialogue between clinical and research.

As an example and reaffirmation of the proposed actions, it can be stated that it has been demonstrated that clinical simulation in nursing has allowed students to develop analysis, synthesis and decision making skills, being this the axis of creation of a pedagogical tool that works on clinical reasoning and facilitates interprofessional education[5] .

Interprofessional health care teams optimize the skills of their members to deliver holistic, patient-centered, high-quality health services. In this regard, the faculty embraces interprofessional education as a necessary step in preparing the health workforce to collaborate and respond to health needs in a dynamic environment.

Faculty preparation is most important for the development of Interprofessional Education as a strategy to strengthen the capacity of human resources for health, improve health outcomes and ultimately strengthen health systems. This requires the creation and use of effective pedagogical tools to facilitate faculty in institutions of Higher Medical Education to undertake this immeasurable but important task.

A system of Interprofessional Education will allow the design of flexible strategies and plans, linked to teaching, the strategic planning of the corresponding organizational unit, linked to the teaching process, the activities of science and technological innovation, university extension, which will contribute to the increase of promotion to main and higher teaching and scientific categories and the obtaining of scientific degrees, which should be reflected in the annual and five-year individual development plans of each professor.

The implementation of Interprofessional Education and Collaborative Practice, in the categorization and promotion of teaching categories, aims at new changes in the teaching-learning process, with strategies for training and qualification of health professionals, which will ensure that:

> The Cuban University of Medical Sciences should become a teaching and scientific center of excellence, capable of responding to the health problems in each territory.
>
> There is greater attention and quality in the processes, which will provide solutions to the problems identified in the health sector, improving the population's health care.
>
> Better preparation of the teaching staff, which will allow for better results in collaboration activities, practice and exchanges with other national and international professionals.
>
> The EIP, facilitates the training of experienced teachers, with higher teaching categories and scientific degrees, which will allow them autonomy in decision making, quality to communicate with responsibility and mastery.

The Universities and Faculties of Medical Sciences have the mission to implement strategies that contribute to the solution of the difficulties detected and to the attainment of the scientific degree in the territories, which includes professors, professionals and the different levels of management of the sector, establishing priorities and measures that allow the increase of Doctors of Science with a proactive vision, to guarantee that research at its highest level participates as a productive social force in the solution of the problems of each territory and of the country in general.

Health systems face a number of challenges in addressing the large gaps and inequalities that threaten the health of the population related to new infectious risks, as well as multiple and complex environmental and behavioral problems, so they need to adapt to a changing reality, with increasing pressure to control costs and increase productivity, while responding to the demands of growing and aging populations, situations of chronicity and the greater complexity of health problems with advanced technologies and more sophisticated consumerism, in addition to the increased specialization of services, the increased professionalization of the different occupational groups and the greater willingness of patients and families to participate as members of the healthcare team.

These changes, which are becoming more evident every day, make it necessary to question the most effective, efficient, effective, safe and quality way of working in healthcare organizations. Specifically, it is proposed that no profession can respond autonomously to all the needs of the patient or to future changes related to demographics and scientific and technological advances, so there are 3 factors that have accentuated the need for teamwork:

A more global conception of the patient

The need to ensure a more specialized and fragmented care continuum

The influence of policies that promote teamwork to achieve quality health care.

F ac tors that have ac tua ted the need for teamwork:

It is therefore logical that among the many challenges present in the reality of work and training in health, training for effective teamwork and collaborative practices, with an integrated approach, user-centered, with strong collaboration between different professional categories and sectors responsible for improving the quality of life and health of people, stands out. This justifies a greater need for interdependence between health and non-health professionals and, consequently, for the so-called interprofessional collaborative practice.

For successful teamwork to be achieved, healthcare professionals must be educated and trained; this is known as Interprofessional Education (IPE).

Interprofessional Education (IPE) is a pedagogical strategy in which members or students of two or more health or social care professions engage in learning with each other, with others and around others; it has been defined as a necessary step for health professionals to be "prepared for collaborative practice", an indispensable dimension to establish teamwork and thus respond to local health needs.

Interprofessional co l abor at i o n a l pr ac tic e

There are multiple definitions of interprofessional collaborative practice (IPP). However, they all communicate a fundamental idea that healthcare is best conducted if it is conceptualized as interprofessional collaboration or teamwork. In short, interprofessional collaborative practice can be defined as a process in which a range of healthcare professionals from different disciplinary **backgrounds** work together to solve problems and participate in decision making, recognizing shared responsibility for outcomes, to provide comprehensive care by working with patients, their families and communities to deliver the highest quality of care in all settings.

In other words, interprofessional collaboration is understood as work in which different health and social professionals work together to solve problems or provide services. On the other hand, we understand that teamwork is an activity in which different professionals participate with a common objective, which in this case would be to provide quality care that favors a rapid and adequate evolution of the patient.

Teamwork is not guaranteed by the creation of formal rules and regulations, and requires people to lead the process in an attractive, creative and dynamic way.

Necessary characteristics and competencies for the interprofessional competitive practice.

There are seven aspects of utmost importance that characterize this health care model:

- Clear description of the responsibilities, roles and limits of each profession towards the others. With the existence of integrated objectives, set objectives and review needs in which all members have the option to actively participate.
- Recognition of the roles, responsibilities and competencies of the members of the interprofessional team. Clear team roles and responsibilities: each member performs his or her role competently and creatively and is aware of the responsibilities and functions of the other professionals on the team.
- Establishment of common goals and individualized care plans for each patient.
- Teamwork to resolve conflicts related to the provision of care and treatment.
- Valuing and tolerating differences and disagreements among professions to improve group performance is based on a timely decision-making strategy, which can be:
  - Unanimously
  - Leaving the decision to the person with the highest scientific level.
  - By majority vote
  - By Consensus, among others
- Planning frequent meetings between team members.
- The establishment of interdependent relationships between professionals from different disciplines.

It follows from the above that, in interprofessional collaborative practice, the different professional groups cease to work independently and in parallel to adopt a common goal and work interdependently. This assumes the premise that the whole is more than the sum of its parts; it is, therefore, the condition and needs of the patient that determine the collaboration and the members of the interprofessional team involved.

Competencies

The following collaborative competencies are considered to be developed by the members of an interprofessional team:

- q Cooperation/collaboration: Collaboration is the most common descriptor of teamwork in healthcare, but are we truly collaborative? There are key principles that establish it:

  Sharing responsibilities, with timely planning, intervention and decision making, based on the Philosophy of health care, from a professional perspective.

  Based on the association of two or more individuals, in a collegial relationship with open and honest communication, mutual trust and respect, where each team member values the work and perspectives of the others, directed towards a common goal or set of shared objectives.

  An interdependence, determined by mutual dependence, interdependent rather than autonomous, where the individual contribution is maximized, so that the result of the whole becomes much greater than the sum of the parts.

  Shared power among team members, so that there is simultaneous empowerment of each participant whose power is recognized by all.
- q Assertiveness
- q Responsibility
- q Open and fluid communication: Developing adequate interprofessional communication results in a complex process, if one keeps in mind that professions have different value systems during the training process. Each of these professional values creates communication barriers between professions. New professionals begin their careers with interprofessional barriers of unfamiliar vocabulary, different approaches to problem solving, and a lack of common understanding of issues and values. Communication skills taught to students usually focus on interactions with patients and families from the perspective of their profession, not on communication across professions. A willingness to collaborate, trust, communicate with others, and demonstrate respect are necessary for collaborative work " Simply bringing people together to work does not necessarily produce an effective working team." Every team needs a clear sense of purpose. A clear sense of what our role is, to be mediators between the Health Center and the community we serve. Therefore, the development of this process requires: developing trusting relationships and active listening, in a way that respects differences of opinion and perspective, good communication in which

dialogue is the basis of the communicative process.
Clear and open communication, in which active listening is an essential part of communication, contributes to good quality care.

- q coordination that establishes appropriate interdependence and integration among team members and their work practices.
- q willingness to share power and leadership. there is recognition by the leader and the rest of the team of individual and collective performance and success.

It is recommended to pay attention not only to competencies, but also to educational processes that integrate a collaborative practice based on knowledge, skills, attitudes and values.

When all the above elements appear simultaneously, the result is an effective collaborative practice in which the benefits are perceived not only in the patient but also in the professionals and in the organization of the healthcare system, with a positive impact on the reduction of the length of hospital stay, mortality, the incidence of complications (e.g. nosocomial infections) and greater continuity of care. On the other hand, for professionals, it translates into an increase in retention and job satisfaction and an improvement in the organizational climate of the teams. Finally, the effects on the efficiency of services and the reduction of healthcare costs should never be forgotten.

Interdisciplinary education for the promotion of interpro fessional collaborative practice

Interdisciplinary Education should address issues to be developed in students:

Teamwork skills.
Communication skills.
Conflict resolution skills.
A certain flexibility in terms of role assignment.
Leadership skills, crucial especially for faculty.

Students in training are rarely given the opportunity to learn effective methods to collaborate with other professionals, develop communication skills and employ teamwork strategies based on respect for others and recognition of the roles and responsibilities of each of the professions. However, it has been recognized that there is a need for students in the medical sciences to be educated not only to provide patient-centered care and evidence-based practice, but also to apply quality improvement, use informatics, and develop interprofessional team practice as ways to improve patient safety.

Pr ác t ica co l abor at i va c entr a t e d i n t h e p aci en t.

It is designed to promote the active participation of each discipline in patient care.

1. Improve patient- and family-centered goals and values.
2. Provides mechanisms for ongoing communication among caregivers
3. Optimizes staff participation in clinical decision making within and across disciplines
4. Encourages respect for the disciplinary contributions of professionals.
5. It occurs when healthcare professionals work within their own profession, with people outside their profession and with patients/clients and their families.
6. It requires a climate of trust and value, where suppliers can comfortably ask questions without worrying about being seen as outsiders.
7. When health care providers are working collaboratively, they pursue common goals and can discuss and resolve any issues that arise.

F ac tors that **f** e **c** t the Interprofessional Cooperation Pr ac tic e

The scientific literature provides evidence that healthcare providers are reluctant to incorporate interprofessional collaborative practice in their workplace. To understand the factors that condition the success or failure of ICP in organizations, multidimensional frameworks must be adopted.

One of the most referenced is the one developed by Reeves et al, where the facilitators and barriers to PCI are grouped into four domains and it is pointed out that, although they occur independently, they are all interconnected.

The relational dimension brings together factors that directly affect the relationships between professionals, such as:

a) power relations,

b) professional hierarchy, from a historical point of view, social recognition has determined that interactions among health professionals are authoritarian and dominated by physicians, however, it is considered that the exclusive predominance of medical power undoubtedly hinders interaction among the team.

c) socialization of norms, values and attitudes associated with each professional group,

d) the professional roles essential for effective relationships and increased team performance, the process of developing professionalization, seeking to belong to a group, building their identity and emulating their teachers as role models to define their roles and practices.

e) communication, both verbal and written, which, if it flows freely and openly, generates more effective attention,

f) trust and respect, increased development, enabling professionals to work in a more integrated way.

Within this dimension, special attention should be paid to the concept of interprofessionalism. One of the problems faced in developing educational activities for interprofessional training is that of communicating the concept of interprofessionality to students, teachers and authorities. It can be observed that the meaning traditionally given to the concept of multidiscipline has a similarity with that of interprofessionality; however, they are two different concepts and the latter is of more recent use. The concept of multidiscipline is rooted in the community, while that of interprofessionalism is not easily incorporated into the language of students and professors.

The processual dimension includes factors related to the way collaborative practices are carried out, such as:

a) the time and space where professionals participate and collaborate in shared activities,

b) routines,

c) information technologies,

d) complexity and

e) delegation of functions.

The organizational dimension refers to those factors that influence and structure the environment in which teams interact, such as organizational support, professional representation and fear of litigation.

And finally, the contextual dimension includes factors related to the social, political and economic landscape in which the team operates, such as culture, diversity, gender, political will and economics.

F igure 2. M arks mu 11 id i mens ion a ls of th e **f** act io n s a ffec ting th e Practic e C o la bora tive Interpro fession 1 (as per Ree **ves** a nd co **ls**)

Dimens ión relacional **Dimensión procesual**

Práctica colaborativa interprofesional

Dimensión organizacional **Dimensión contextual**

Interprofessional Collaborative Practice and Primary Health Care

In the course of the last decades, the concept of Interprofessional Collaborative Practice has become increasingly important both in academic contexts and in health care facilities. This relevance was accompanied by a modification in the conception of Public Health and its care. In the first place, a change in the conception of health was evidenced, where health has ceased to mean the absence of disease and has progressively become synonymous with "quality of life", "wellbeing", "healthy environment", etc.

Secondly, and based on this redefinition of the concept of health, a differentiation of the levels of care is established, where the discrimination between promotion, prevention, primary, secondary and tertiary health care and their application in different devices becomes particularly important.

These changes in Health Systems were largely driven by the directives established by the World Health Organization (WHO). A key event in this direction was the Alma-Ata declaration, which established certain guidelines for the development of the health system, including Primary Health Care (PHC), which will be defined from this point on as "the central function and the main core" of the national health system.

Primary Health Care (PHC) is conceived as the gateway to the health system: as the contact area between communities and health centers. This is where the creation of a professional team capable of responding to the different demands of the population becomes important.

It is within this framework that the work necessarily implies interprofessional collaborative practice, since accompanying this complexization of health care is another conception of the person and his/her suffering that does not take refuge in linear or unicausal explanations and therefore requires an interdisciplinary approach where the different disciplines will not constitute a simple juxtaposition, but a common construction of the problem to be addressed, with delimitation of the different levels of analysis and the configuration of care teams that aim at the production of concrete actions in common.

Pl an if icat ion of Interprofessional C o la bora tive Practice in Primary Health Care (PHC)

A clear and recognizable idea or goal must serve as the focus for team members for teamwork to succeed.

Each member should change his or her professional focus to one that requires an understanding of the observations and interpretations of others.

Collaborative Practice should provide a level playing field among the various members of the team.

A well-designed goal should be SMART.

Specific. Specific

Measurable - Measurable

Achievable - Alcanzable

Reliable - Reliable

Time-limited - Limited time

A team approach to healthcare decreases work frustration and increases efficiency.

Increases staff satisfaction and retention.

Collaboration, while vital for organizations to function, is often lacking in member performance evaluations.

R esu lts and Benefits of Interprofessional Cooperative Practices

More and more research indicates that it contributes to the improvement of the quality and safety of clinical care, in aspects such as:

Increasing patient satisfaction and reducing patient and family complaints by ensuring timely patient safety.

Appropriate management of chronic diseases

Reduction of costs, mortality rates, complications and clinical errors.

Reduction of waiting time for clinical stays and duplication of efforts.

Reducing stress and burnout of professionals by creating or maintaining healthy workplaces, through the use of appropriate language when speaking with other health care professionals providers or patients/family, understanding that all health care providers contribute to the collaborative team or unit.

Introducing new team members in a way that is welcoming and gives them the information they need to be a contributing member

Increased job satisfaction for professionals by showing respect and building trust among team members and mutual support when mistakes are made and celebrating together when success is achieved.

Retention of professionals in the institutions and reduction of their turnover, stabilizing the availability of human resources in health.

Figure 3. Different Health Care Models

Practices For the

Individual disciplines Health assessment Plan of care

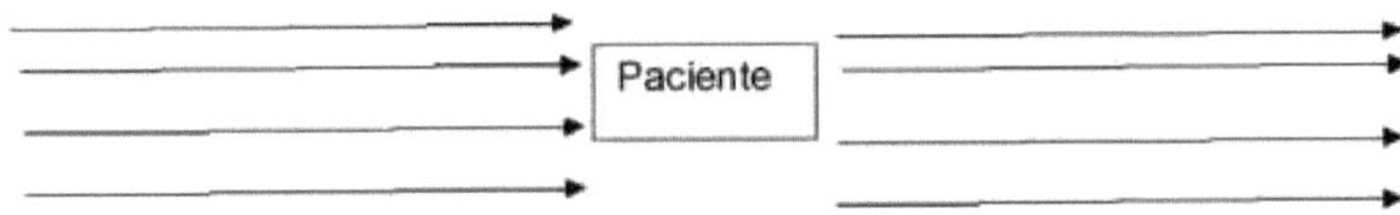

Minimal communication between disciplines

Mu lt i d isc ip linar y pr ac tics

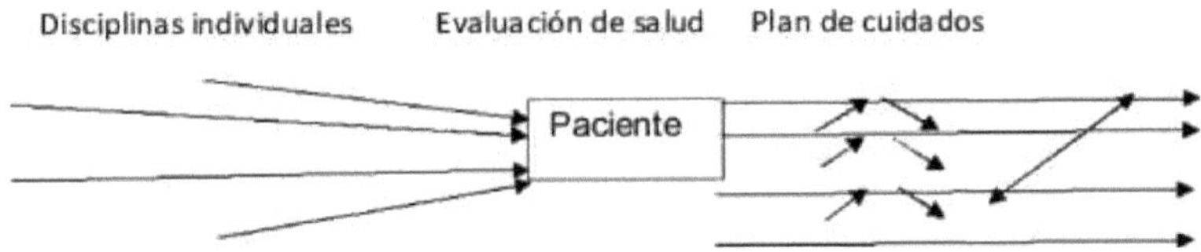

Increases collaboration and communication between disciplines

Interpro fessional Co la bor at ive Pr ac tic ics

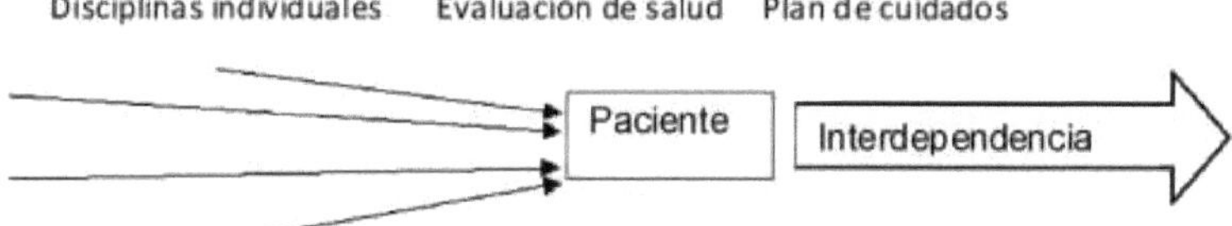

Interdependence in the decisions made by disciplines

What are the challenges that remain for the coordina t ive pract ice? Pending challenges.

Currently, in clinical practice, health management and health education, the dominant and hierarchical role of medicine in relation to the other health disciplines continues to be naturalized, in most cases without questioning, which distances us from an integrative, integrative and collaborative perspective. In order to improve the effectiveness and efficiency of health teams, interventions that promote mutual recognition of complementarity and interdependence are necessary, such as the creation of horizontal management structures and the promotion of activities that encourage collaboration, communication and joint decision-making between nurses, physicians and other health professionals.

The evidence also recommends other types of interventions, such as interprofessional health education, both in undergraduate and postgraduate training and in continuing education, that promote the perspective of patient-centered care, interprofessional communication, interdisciplinary rounds or interprofessional approach protocols. Interventions to promote PCI, whose efficacy has been demonstrated, have in common to dissipate professional differences and focus on building alliances, cooperation and healthy forms of leadership with the aim of ensuring safe care and generating greater innovation and progress in health services.

Interprofessionalism is defined as the development of collaborative practice among health care providers from different professions. During this process, professionals reflect and develop forms of practice to provide a comprehensive response to the needs of patients, families and communities. Interprofessionalism requires a paradigm shift, as interprofessional practice has particular characteristics, values, codes of conduct and ways of working.

The concept of interprofessionalism would allow the establishment of educational programs that facilitate the formation of well-communicated health care teams with ethical values and behaviors and that respect the roles of the different professions involved. Participants in interprofessional education exercises often recognize the benefits of being able to communicate effectively and respectfully with members of other professions and better value the contributions they can make from the point of view of their own, understanding the specific roles of each of the team members.

BIBLIOGRAPHY

Balaguer Cabrera JR. Ministry of Public Health. Projections of Public Health in Cuba for 2015. (Brochure) Havana, Cuba: MINSAP; 2006. p 7-42.

Barr. H. and Low. H. Center for the Advancement of Interprofessional Education (CAIPE).2013.

Cañizares Luna. O. "Dr. Serafín Ruiz de Zarate Ruiz" Higher Institute of Medical Sciences of Villa Clara. 2000

C **arre ño de** C **elis**. R. Ministry of Public Health. Teaching and Research Area. 2002

Díaz Quiñones JA, Considerations for the improvement of the teaching-learning process in Higher Medical Education. Medisur [Journal of medical sciences on the Internet]. 2015 [cited 23 Jan 2016]; 13 (5):[approx. 6p]. Available from: http://medisur.sld.cu/index.php/me disur/article/article/view/3133.

F **e rnández** O liv a. B. National School of Public Health. Havana. 2004

Ilizástigui Dupuy F. Higher Medical Education and the health needs of the population (Brochure) Ministry of Public Health, Havana: 1993: p-11-22.

Morales Villavicencio. CE. Oramas Gonzalez. R. Valcarcel Izquierdo. N. Rodriguez Rensoli. M. Cuenca Ecuador. 2015

Ministerial Resolution 111 issued for the Higher Education Teaching Organization Regulations by the Ministry of Higher Education. 2017

Ministerial Resolution 2 issued for the Regulation of Teaching and Methodological Work in Higher Education by the Ministry of Higher Education. 2018

Study plans of the careers in the area of Health Technologies. Ministry of Public Health. 2010

Study plan of the Medicine career. Ministry of Public Health. 2014

Salas Perea RS. Educación en Salud: Competencia y Desempeño profesionales. Editorial Ciencias Médicas. Havana, 1999. p- 27-51.

AGUIRRE CÁRDENAS, JESÚS. Formación pedagógica y didácticas universitarias. http//www.nhc.noaa.gov/ftp/graphiscs/ATB/AL 1302 W.GIF. 6 p.

BARRIOS, R. OSCAR. La formación docente: Theory and practice . Pedagogical Information Center. Metropolitan University of Educational Sciences. 6 p. 2001

BREHM B, BREEN P, BROWN B, et al. An interdisciplinary approach to introducing professionalism. Am J Pharm Ed uc. 2006; 70:81.

BEUNZA J, Manual of Interprofessional Health Education. Elsevier. European University of Madrid. 2018. Available at: http://tienda. elsevier.es/manual-de-educación-interprofesional-sanitaria-9788491132 967.html.

BEUNZA J, Interview at the II Jornada Nacional de Educación Interprofesional: "Promoting health collaboration". European University of Madrid. 2018.

Available at: https://www.elsevier.com/
_data/assets/pdf_file/0019/727003/porgrms_jornadaseip_2018.pdf
CASCANTE, C. General Didactics Teaching Project. University of Oviedo. Unpublished. 1996
Cáceres, M. et al: The pedagogical training of university teachers. Iberoamerican Journal of Education (ISSN: 1681-5653).
CARR, W; KEMMIS, S. Critical teaching theory. Action research in teacher education. Editora Martínez Roca. Barcelona. 1998
Centre for the Advancement of Interprofessional Education (CAIPE). Available from: http ://www.ca ipe.o rg.uk/about-us/defi ning-ipe/?keywords=defin ition. Accessed 2009 Aug 18.
(COLLECTIVE OF AUTHORS. MINED.) Documentos normativos para el perfeccionamiento del Sistema Nacional de Educación. Editorial Pueblo y Educación. Ciudad de La Habana. 1998
DEL CARMEN, L. Curriculum development and in-service teacher training. In Gil Pérez. 1990
Training of trainers in Science Didactics. Editorial Nau Llibres. Valencia. 1990 p 45-48
DE LELLA, CAYETANO. Models and trends in teacher education. I Seminario Taller sobre perfil del docente y estrategias de formación. Lima, Perú. 1999. 9 p.
FERNÁNDEZ PÉREZ, M. La profesionalización docente en la escuela. Escuela español. S.A. Madrid. 1988
GIROUX, H. A. Teachers as intellectuals. Ediciones Paidós/MEC. Barcelona. 1990
GONZÁLEZ, OTMARA. El enfoque histórico cultural como fundamento de una concepción pedagógica. Tendencias Pedagógicas Contemporáneas. Collective of authors. University of Havana. CEPES. Ciudad de La Habana 1991. 92-114 p.
IGLESIAS LEÓN, MIRIAM ET AL. The pedagogical preparation of university professors. Its impact on the quality of Higher Education. Paper presented at the 3rd International Convention on Higher Education. University 2002. 12 p.
SILVA FAM, CASSIANI SHDB, FILHO JRF. The PAHO/WHO Regional Network of Interprofessional Health Education. Rev. Latino-Am. Enfermagem. 2018; 26: e3013. Available in: DOI: http:// dx.doi.org/10.1590/1518-8345.0000.3013
WORLD HEALTH ORGANIZATION Framework for Action on Interprofessional Education & Collaborative Practice 2010 :12-31.
WORLD HEALTH ORGANIZATION. Global strategy for human resources for health: health workforce 2030. WHO; 2014. Available at: http://apps.who.int/gb/ebwha/pdf_files/WHA69/A69_38-sp. pdf.
PAN AMERICAN HEALTH ORGANIZATION. Interprofessional education in health care: improving human resources capacity to achieve universal health. Report of the December 7-9, 2016 meeting in Bogotá, Colombia. Washington, D.C.: PAHO;

2017.
Regional Network for Interprofessional Education in the Americas. [REIP]. [Internet]. [cited March 13, 2018]. 2018. Available from: http://www.educacioninterprofesional.org/red-regional-de-educacion-interprofessional-of-the-americas
KYRKJEBO JM, BRATTEBO G, SMITH-STROM H. Improving patient safety by using interprofessional simulation training in health professional education. J Interprof Care. 2006; 20:507-516.
Alarcón Ortiz, Rodolfo. Cuban Higher Education: Quality, impact, and main challenges Speech by the Minister of Higher Education, delivered in Angola July 2013.
Collective of authors. Diagnosis of the management process of teaching categories at the University of Sancti Spíritus "José Martí Pérez". Cuba.
Baute, L. M., & Iglesias, M. (2011). Systematization of a pedagogical experience: university teacher training. Pedagogía Univ ersitari a, 16 (1), pp.36-49.
Esquivel, R. (2008 and 2012). Variable Form **e** 2 **Human Resources** Management for Inst itu **ti** ona l Ev a l u a t i o n Univ **e** rs idad **de** Sane ti ti Spíri **tus** " J **osé** Mart í **Pér ez**".
Fat Aguillón, G. (2011). Didactic actions oriented to the change of teaching category in municipal university centers (CUM) Part I. **Cuadernos de** Educ ación y D **esarro** llo, 3 (24), 56-72.
Hernández, S., Fernández, C., & Baptista, L. (2006). Metodología **de** la investigación. Fourth edition.
Imbernón, F. (2000). La formaci ón y **e** l d esarrollo **profes** ional del **profe** sor. Barcelona: Grao.
Centre for the Advancement of Interprofessional Education (CAIPE).Defining IPE.[Internet]. 2002 [cited 12 Nov 2017] [approx. 10 p.]. Available from: http://www.caipe.org.uk/about-us/defining-ipe.
McFadyen AK, Maclaren WM, Webster VS. The Interdisciplinary Education Perception Scale (IEPS): An alternative remodeled sub-scale structure and its reliability. RevInterprofCare.2007; 21(4):433-443.
Curran VR, Sharpe D, Forristall J, Flynn K. Attitudes of health sciences students towards interprofessional teamwork and education. RevLearnHealthSocCare. 2008; 7:146-56.
World Health Organization.(WHO) Framework for Action on Interprofessional Education and Collaborative Practice.Geneva, WHO, [Internet]. 2010 [cited14 Sep 2017] [approx. 10 p.]. Available from:
http://www.who.int/hrh/resources/framework_action/en/.

Wilhelmsson M, Pelling S, Uhlin L, Dahlgren LO, Faresjo T, Forslund K. How to think about Interprofessional competence: A metacognitive model. Rev Interprof Care. 2012;26:85-91

NOrgaard B, Dragborg E, Vestergaard E, Odgaard E, Jensen DC, SOrensen J. Interprofessional clinical training improves self-efficacy of health care students. Rev Med Teach. 2013; 35:1235-1242.

Michalec B, Giordano C, Arenson C, Antony R, Rose M. Dissecting first-year students' perceptions of health profession groups: potential barriers to interprofessional education. J AlliedHealth. 2013; 42(4):202-213.

Leikas S, Salmela-Aro K. Personality Trait Changes Among Young Finns: The Role of Life Events and T ransitionsJ Pers. 2015; 83:117-126.

Soto Fuentes P. From interprofessional education to teamwork in health. Santiago de Chile: Pontificia Universidad Católica de Chile; 2017.

Arango AM, Ariza Montoya JF, Zambrano A. Interprofessional health education (IPE) in Colombia. Avances. [Internet]. 2018 [cited 12 Nov 2018] [approx. 10 p.]. Available from: file:///F:/.
education%20inter%20professional/education%20interprofessional/12.francisco_m ontoya_col.pdf

González Pascual et al. Interprofessional education through home care: experience after two years of implementation. European University of Madrid. Medical Education. [Internet]. 2018 [cited 12 Nov 2018] [approx. 10 p.]. Available from: www.elsevier.es/ edumed

Espina Prieto, M. Complexity and social thought. Complexus. Journal of Complexity, Science and Aesthetics . [Internet]. 2005 [cited 12 Nov 2017] [approx. 10 p.]. Available from: http://www.sintesys.cl/complexus/revista2/
articles2/maira%20spina.pdf

Macías Llanes, ME. Tensions in the epistemological treatment of health. In: Humanidades Médicas. No 3. [Internet]. 2001 [cited 12 Nov 2017] [approx. 10 p.]. D i spo nible en: http ://bvs.sld.cu/revistas/revistahm/numeros/.
2001/n3/art/art02.htm

Macías Llanes ME. Social studies of science and technology in the field of health: an experience in graduate education. Havana: Editorial Félix Varela; 2002.

Central Committee of the Communist Party of Cuba. Documents VI Congress of the PCC. Resolution on ideological political work. Havana: Editora Política; 2010.

Central Committee of the Communist Party of Cuba. VI Congress of the PCC. Lineamientos de la política económica y social del Partido y la Revolución. Havana: Editora Política; 2011.

Central Committee of the Communist Party of Cuba. First National Conference of the PCC. Objectives for the ideological political work. Havana: Editora Política; 2012.

Central Committee of the Communist Party of Cuba. VII Congress of the PCC. Actualización de los Lineamientos de la política económica y social del Partido y la Revolución. Havana: Editora Política; 2016.
Central Committee of the Communist Party of Cuba. VII Congress of the PCC. Strategic axis: Human development, equity and justice, Specific Objectives 197. 3 and 200. 6. Havana: Editora Política; 2016.
Robinson Jay F, Ramos Duharte D. Sociohumanistic competence: an essential component of the health professional. Journal of Scientific Information. [Internet]. 2016 [cited 2016 Nov 12] [approx. 10 p.]. Available from: http://www.gtm. sld.cu/imagen/ RIC/Vol 95 No.6/.
Guerrero, Manuel A. "Keys to the successful leader". Published in Hernández Sampieri, R.; Fernández Collado, C. Y Baptista, P. Metodología de la Investigación. Mexico: Editora Publi-Mex. S.A; 1995.
Fernández David, S.J. New paradigms for a humanistic education. [Internet]. 2012 [cited 10 Jul 2016]: [approx. 12 p]. Available from: http:// www.gdl. iteso.mx/event/
Del Huerto Marimón, M E. University extension from a strategic perspective in the integral management of the contemporary medical university. Rev.Educ Med Super. 2012; 26 (4):
Castro Sánchez F. University, Innovation and Society: global processes and the Cuban experience. [Doctoral Thesis]. University of Matanzas "Camilo Cienfuegos. 2007.
Figaredo Curiel, F. (2002): Aims of science-technology-society education in Cuba. [Doctoral dissertation]. University of Havana; 2002.
World Conference on Science for the 21st Century: A New Commitment. Budapest Declaration. Declaration on Science and the Use of Scientific Knowledge. UNESCO-ICSU. Budapest (Hungary) from June 26 to July 1, 1999.
Castellanos, B. et al (2003). Aproximación a un marco conceptual para la investigación educativa. In: Collective of authors. Methodology of educational research. Desafíos y polémicas actuales. Havana: Editorial Pueblo y Educación; 2003.
Central Committee of the Communist Party of Cuba. VII Congress of the PCC. Update of the Guidelines of the economic and social policy of the Party and the Revolution for the period 2016-2021. Havana: Editora Política; 2016.
VII Congress of the PCC. National Economic and Social Development Plan until 2030: Vision of the Nation, Strategic Axes and Sectors. Strategic axis: Human development, equity and justice, Specific objectives 200. 6. Havana: Editora Política; 2016.
Ministry of Public Health. Necessary Transformations of the Public Health System. Havana: Ciencias Médica Publishing House; 2010.

Macías Llanes ME. Education in Science-Technology-Society in the general comprehensive training of the health professional . Havana: Editorial de Ciencias Médicas; 2012.
Central Committee of the Communist Party of Cuba. First National Conference of the PCC. Objectives for the ideological political work. Havana: Editora Política; 2012.
Izaguirre Remón, RC. The socio-medical cosmovisational competence as a didactic construct for the training of the basic comprehensive general practitioner. [Doctoral Thesis]. CEES Manuel F Gran. Universidad de Oriente; 2007 p33
López Dosagües R. The philosophy of the uses of sociohumanistic knowledge: trajectory in Cuba between 1959 and 2009. [Doctoral dissertation]. University of Havana: CEES; 2015.
Robinson Jay F. Sociohumanistic Competence in Health Care Professionals. Düsseldorf, Germany: Editorial Académica Española; 12 January 2018. ISBN 978620-2-25177-8. 150p
Castell-FloritSerrate P. Intersectoriality in the social practice of the Cuban public health system. [Havana: ENSAP, 2004.
Oliva B, Morales Suárez I and Portal Pineda J. System of influences for the integral formation of the graduates of the centers of Higher Medical Education. RevEducMedSuper. [Internet]. 2004. [cited 10 Jul 2017]. [approx. 10 p]. Available from: http: //bvs.sld.cu/revistas/ems/vol18_2_04/ems02204.htm.
World Health Organization: Proposed Strategies for Assessing Health Systems Performance. [Internet]. 2010 [cited 10 December 2013] [approx. 9 p.]. Available from: http://www.who.int/health.systems-perfor mance/prerreview doc/sprgspanish.pdf.
García Capote J. Curricular redesign of the discipline philosophy and health science for the integral and humanistic development of medical science graduates. [Doctoral dissertation]. Havana: University of Medical Sciences; 2014.
Añorga Morales J. Pedagogy and Didactic and Curricular Strategy of Advanced Education. Havana: Editorial Pueblo y Educación; 1995.
Valle Lima AD. Pedagogical Research. Otra Mirada. Havana: Editorial Pueblo y Educación; 2010. 197 - 205.
Sosa Sánchez TM. Pedagogical strategy for the improvement of medical performance of specialists in training in internal medicine in the comprehensive care of epileptic patients and their families. [Doctoral Thesis]. Havana: "Enrique José Varona" University of Pedagogical Sciences; 2016.
Freire P. Pedagogy of autonomy. [Internet]. 2008 [cited 26 Oct 2017]; [ca. 70 p]. Available at: https://practicasdelaen2.files.word press.com /2016/07/freire-pedagogc3ada-de-la-autonomc3ada.pdf.
Pla López R. Pedagogy as a science from the cultural historical approach. Result of

the research project "Pedagogy". Havana: Sello Editorial. Educación; 2011.

Castellanos D. and Coauthors. Learning and teaching in school. Una concepción desarrolladora. Havana: Editorial Pueblo y Educación. First reprint; 2013.

Izquierdo Hernández AA. Methodology for the dynamics of professional development in the health sector. [Doctoral Thesis]. University of Oriente: CEES Manuel F Grant; 2008.

Pernas Gómez M. et al. Methodological model for the design and application of curricular strategies in Medical Sciences. Rev. Educ. Med Super. [Internet]. 2010 Jan-Mar. [cited 10 Dec. 2013]; 24(1): [approx. 9 p.]. Available from: http://scielo.sld.cu/scielo. php?script=sci_arttext&pid=S0864-21412010000 100005&lng=en&nrm=iso&tlng=en.

Borroto Cruz ER, Lemus Lago ER. Trends in medical education training programs. [Internet]. 2014[cited 12 Jun 2015]. [approx.5p.]. Available from: http://conferenciasiglo21.sld.cu/index.php/confe renciasiglo21/2014/paper/view/572/84.

Fernández Sacasa E. Contemporary trends in Higher Medical Education. [Internet]. 2013 [cited 12 Jun 2015]. [approx. 10p.]. Available from: http://edumedhabana.sld.cu/index.php/edumedhabana/2013/paper/viewFile / 249/228.

Addine Fernández, F. Didactics and optimization of the teaching-learning process. Havana: Editorial Pueblo y Educación; 1998.

Miranda T. The didactics of higher education. In: La didáctica de la formación de formadores: resultados teóricos y experiencias prácticas. Havana: Pedagogía 2011, Volume 15. 2011.

González Soca AM. [et al.] The teaching-learning process a challenge for change. In Didactics theory and practice. Havana: Editorial Pueblo y Educación, 2011.

Sierra Figueredo S. Curricular strategies in Higher Education: their projection in undergraduate and graduate Higher Medical Education. Rev. Educ Med Super. [Internet]. 2009 [cited 10 Jul. 2016]; 23(3): [approx. 11 p]. Available from: http://scielo.sld.cu/scielo.php?script=sci_arttext&pid= S0864

Viñedo Tomey A. The integration of knowledge in medical education.Rev Educ Med Superior. [Internet]. 2009.[cited 13 May 2015]; 23(4): [ca. p.10]. Available from: http://scielo.sld.cu/scielo.php?script= sciarttext&pid= S0864 - Esteban M. Introduction to the study of learning strategies and learning styles. Journal of Distance Education. No 17. [Internet]. 2013 [cited 10 Jul 2015]. [approx.10p]. Available from: http://www.um.es/ead/ red/6/documento6.pdf .

Elias Sierra, R. Una metodología para el desarrollo de la habilidad atención médica integral en el médico general en formación inicial [Doctoral thesis]. Havana: Central Institute of Pedagogical Sciences; 2015.

Bernaza Rodríguez G, Guerra Hernández A, Estrada Sentí V, Pichardo Martínez, R.

The graduate student in conditions of universalization of graduate education: a look from their learning strategies. Havana: Editorial de Ciencias Sociales; 2013.

Carreras Barnés J, Branda LA, Castro Salomó A. Guide for the evaluation of competencies in Medicine. Barcelona: Agencia per a la Qualitat del Sistema Universitari de Catalunya. [Internet]. 2009 [cited 10 Jul 2015]. [approx.292p]. Available from: http://www.aqu. cat/doc/doc_71595240_1.pdf.

Durand Rill R. Model for the development of communicative competence in the educational management process. [Doctoral dissertation]. Santiago de Cuba: Latin American and Caribbean Pedagogical Institute; 2010.

Izaguirre Remón, R. An approach to university extension in Cuban higher medical education. University Congress 2015. [Internet]. 2015 [cited 13 May 2016]; IV (3): [approx. 15 p] Available from: http:// www.congresouniversidad.cu/revista/index.php/co ngresouniversidad/article/view File/1105/553.

Galimany Masclans J, Garrido Aguilar E, Estrada Masllorens JM, Girbau García MR. Training of health professionals in a care context with the use of information and communication technologies. FEM [Internet]. 2013 [cited 26 Oct 2017]; 16(3):127-130. Available from: http://scielo.isciii.es/ pdf/fem/v16n3/co laboracion.pdf.

Ministry of Higher Education. Ministerial Resolution 132-04 of the Regulation of Postgraduate Education. Havana: Ministry of Higher Education; 2004. Collective of authors. Programa del médico y enfermera de la familia. Havana: ECIMED, 2011.

Cuba. Ministry of Higher Education. Ministerial Resolution 2-18 of the Regulation of Methodological Work in Higher Education. Official Gazette. Havana: Editora del Consejo de Estado; 2018.

Macías Llanes M E. Postgraduate training in Science-Technology-Society in the health sector. Results of a training to professors of Medical Humanities Rev. Hum Med v.6 n.3 Ciudad de Camagüey Sep.-Dec. 2010. ISSN 17278120.

Fernández Sacasa E. Contemporary trends in Higher Medical Education. [Internet]. 2013 [cited 12 Jun 2015]. [approx. 10p.]. Available from: http://edumedhabana.sld.cu/index.php/edumedhabana/2013/paper/viewFile /249/ 228.

Montes de Oca Recio N and Machado Ramírez EF. Training and development of competencies in Cuban higher education. Rev Hum Med [Internet]. 2014 [cited 10 Jul 2017]; 14(1):145-159. Available from: http://scielo.sld. cu/pdf/h mc/v14n1/hmc10114.pdf.

Artiles Visval L, Otero Iglesias J, Barrios Osuna I. Research Methodology for Health Sciences. Havana, Cuba: Ecimed; 2009.

Bustamante Alfonso, L. The improvement for teachers linked to the preparation of cadres and health reserves. Thesis in option to the degree of doctor in pedagogical sciences. 2012

Cáceres Diéguez, 2011. Postgraduate Professional Development in Primary Health Care, a didactic strategy for the modification of behaviors and behaviors in favor of healthy lifestyles. Santiago de Cuba.

Lescaille Elias, N. Master's thesis in Educational Sciences. Technical and Professional Education. Design of the diploma course in diagnostic ultrasound, for graduates in health technology, profile Imaging. 2010

Lescaille Elias, N. Performance shown by Health Technology Graduates, Imaging profile, in the diagnostic ultrasound technique. ISSN 22186719. RNPS: 2252. Vol.3, Núm.3 (2012) Cuba. http://www.revtecnologia .sld.cu/ Lescaille Elias, N. Improvement strategy for the improvement of the performance of Health Technology Graduates, Imaging profile, in the diagnostic ultrasound technique, with a practical materialistic conception. ISSN: 2007-7890. Year III. Article #12 Period: June-September 2015. Cuba. Available in: http://www.dilemascontemporaneoseducacionpoliticayvalores.co m/

Portal Pineda, Julio Antonio. V Anniversary of the Health Technologist Training Program. [WEB base-Data]. SCIELO. Available at: http://scielo.sld.cu/scielo.php?script=sci arttext&pid=S1729-519X2008000100001&lng=en&nrm=iso&tlng=en

Ramos Suárez, V. Lescaille Elias, N. Proposal for mammography training for imaging technologists. Cuba Salud 2015. International Health Convention. Cuba. Editorial ECIMED. ISBN: 978-959-212-963-4. Available at: http://actasdecongreso.sld.cu/

Izquierdo Hernández, Asunción. Methodology for the dynamics of Professional Improvement in the Health Sector. Thesis presented in option to the scientific degree of Doctor in Pedagogical Sciences. 2008

Valcárcel N et al. Project: "Estrategia de Superación Conjunta de la Dirección Provincial de Educación de Ciudad de La Habana, el ISPEJV y la Escuela" (Joint Improvement Strategy of the Provincial Directorate of Education of Havana City, the ISPEJV and the School). Result # 1: "Essential relations of the Improvement Strategy (Conceptual Framework)". Higher Pedagogical Institute "Enrique José Varona". Faculty of Education Sciences. Chair of Advanced Education. Havana City, July 2001. p.3.

Valcárcel Izquierdo, Norberto. Estrategia Interdisciplinaria de Superación para profesores de Ciencias de la Enseñanza Media. 1998. Thesis presented in option to the Scientific Degree of Doctor in Pedagogical Sciences. Havana.

Interprofessional Education Collaborative (2016). Core competencies for interprofessional collaborative practice: 2016 update. Washington, DC: Interprofessional Education Collaborative.

Batista, N.A and Batista, S.H. (2016.). Interprofessionaleducation in theteaching of thehealthprofessions: shapingpractices and knowledgenetworks. Interface

(Botucatu), 20 (56). DOI: 10.1590/1807-57622015.0388.

Muller-Juge V, Cullati S, Blondon KS, Hudelson P, Maître F, Vu NV, et al. Interprofessionalcollaborationbetweenresidentsand nurses in general internal medicine: a qualitativestudyonbehavioursenhancingteamworkquality. PloSOne. 2014;9(4): e96160.

WorldHealthOrganization. Global strategyon human resourcesforhealth: workforce 2030 [Internet]. Geneva; 2016. [cited Nov 30, 2018]. Availablefrom: http://who.int/hrh/resources/pub globstrathrh-2030/en/

Lie, D.A, Forest, C.P, Walsh, A., Banzali, Y., & Lohenry, K. (2016). What and how do studentslearn in aninterprofessionalstudent-run clinic? Aneducationalframeworkforteam-basedcare. Medical Education Online, 5 (21), 31900.

Roberts, C., &Kumar, K. (2015). Student learning in interprofessionalpractice-basedenvironments: whatdoestheorysay? BMC Medical Education, 15(1), 211. https://doi.org/10.1186/s12909-015-0492-1

Canadian InterprofessionalHealthCollaborative. A nationalinterprofessionalcompetencyframework; February 2010. Availablefrom: http://www.cihc.ca/files/CIHC_IPCompetencies_ Feb1210.pdf Fahs D., Honan L., Gonzalez-Colaso R., ColsonE. Interprofessionaleducationdevelopment: notforthefaintofheart.Advances in Medical Education and Practice. 2017; 8:329-336.

Soto Fuentes P. From interprofessional education to teamwork in health. HorizEnferm, 2017, 28(1):3-6.

Bridges, D.R, Davidson, R.A, Odegard, P.S., Maki, I.V. and Tomkowiak, J. (2011). Interprofessionalcollaboration: threebestpracticemodels of interprofessionaleducation. Medical Education Online, 16, 6035. DOI: 10.3402/meo.v16i0.6035.

Frenk, J., Chen, L., Bhutta, Z.A., Cohen, J., Crisp, N., Evans, T., Fineberg, H., Garcia, P.J., Ke, Y., Kelley, P., Kistnasamy, B., Meleis, A., Naylor, D., Pablos- Mendez, A., Reddy, S., Scrimsaw, S., Sepulveda, J., Serwadda, D. and Zurayk, H. (2015). Health professionals for the new century: transforming education to strengthen health systems in an independent world. Medical Education, 16 (1), 9-16.

Paradis, E., Reeves, S., Leslie, M., Puntillo, K., Gropper, M., Aboumatar, H. J., &Kitto, S. (2014). Deliveringinterprofessionalcare in intensivecare: A scopingreview of ethnographicstudies. American Journal of CriticalCare, 23(3), 230-238. doi:10.4037/ajcc2014155.

Poirier, T., & Wilhelm, M. (2014). Aninterprofessionalfacu ltyseminarfocusedoninterprofessionaleducation. American Journal of PharmaceuticalEducation, 78 (4), 80. http ://doi.org/10.5688/ajpe78480.

Reeves, S., Mcmillan, S. E., Kachan, N., Paradis, E., Leslie, M., Kitto, S., ... Kitto, S. (2015). Interprofessional collaboration and family memberinvolvement in intensivecareunits: emergingthemesfrom a multi-sitedethnography Interprofessional collaboration and family memberinvolvement in intensivecareunits: emerging themesfrom a multi-sit, 1820(May 2016). doi:10.3109/13561820.2014.955914.

Paradis, E., Reeves, S., Leslie, M., Aboumatar, H., Chesluk, B., Clark, P. ... Kitto, S. (2014). Exploring thenature of interprofessional collaboration and family memberin volvement in anintensivecarecontext. Journal of InterprofessionalCare, 28(1), 74-75. doi:10.3109/13561820.2013.781141 Reeves, S. (2016). Whyweneeded interprofessional education to improvethedelivery of safe and effective care. Interface - Comunicação, Saúde, Educação, 20(56), 185-197.

Zaforteza, C., García-Mozo, A., Amorós, S. M., Pérez, E., Maqueda, M., & Delgado, J. (2014). Factors limiting and facilitating changes in caringfortheintensivecareunitpatients' relatives. Nursing in CriticalCare. doi:10.1111/nicc.12095.

Rose, L. (2011). Interprofessional collaboration in theicu: how to define? British Association of Critical Care Nurses, 16(1), 5-10. Retrievedfrom http://web.a.ebscohost.com/ehost/pdfviewer/pdfviewer?sid=0c1f5376-589e-4a4e-9ca2-6df2694f81f6%40sessionmgr4003&vid=20&hid=4212

Reeves, S., Perrier, L., Goldman, J., Freeth, D., &Zwarenstein, M. (2013). Interprofessional education: effectson professional practice and health careoutcomes (update) (Review) SUMMARY OF FINDINGS FOR THE MAIN COMPARISON,(3).
doi:10.1002/14651858.CD002213.pub3.www.cochranelibrary.com

Matziou, V, Vlahioti, E, Perdikaris, P, Matziou, T, Megapanou, E, &Petsios, K. (2014). Physician and
nursingperceptionsconcerninginterprofessionalcommunication and
collaboration. Journal of Interprofessional Care. Journal of Interprofessional Care, 28(6), 526-33.
Retrievedfro mhttp ://doi.org/10.3109/13561820.2014.934338

Luetsch, K., &Rowett, D. (2015). Interprofessional communication training: benefits to practicing pharmacists. International Journal of Clinical Pharmacy, 37(5), 857-64. doi:10.1007/s11096-015-0130-3.

Lifchez, S. D., Cooney, C. M., & Redett, R. J. (2015). The Standardized Professional Encounter: A New Model to Assess Professionalism and Communication Skills. Journal of Graduate Medical Education, 7(2), 230-3. doi:10.4300/JGME-D-14-00275.1.

Haddara, W., &Lingard, L. (2013). Are weallon thesame page? A discourseanalysis of interprofessional collaboration. Academic Medicine: Journal of the Association of American Medical Colleges, 88(10), 1509-15. doi:10.1097/ACM.0b013e3182a31893.

Costa, D. K., Barg, F. K., Asch, D. A., &Kahn, J. M. (2014). Facilitators of an Interprofessional Approach to Care in Medical and Mixed Medical / Surgical! CUs: A Multicenter Qualitative Study. Research in Nursing &Health, 37, 326335. doi:10.1002/nur.21607.

Bengoechea Calpe, L., Marín Fernández, B., &Regaira Martínez, E. (2016). Analysis of the intensity of professional collaboration between nurses in a critical care area. Enfermería Intensiva, 27(2), 44-50.
doi:10.1016/j.enfi.2015.12.001

FERRADAVIDELA, M. (2005). The determinants of successfulcollaboration: A review of theoretical and empiricalstudies. Journal of InterprofessionalCare, 5 (Suppl. 1), 132-147.

Tang CJ, Chan SW, Zhou WT, Liaw SY. Collaborationbetween hospital physicians and nurses: anintegratedliteraturereview. IntNurs Rev. 2013;60: 291-302.

Printed by Books on Demand GmbH, Norderstedt / Germany